With a background in quality assurance and risk management, before specialising in data protection, as well as almost two decades in social housing, Clare Paterson has a holistic understanding of both the business risks and people-centered risks connected to data, and helps people to identify and control these risks, while continually expanding her own knowledge.

Clare is committed to providing the support she knows those working with data need, from her own experience, and does this as the founder of the Hive, a free online group for data professionals in values-led sectors, and the Hive Live, an in-person conference with interactive workshops as well as expert speakers, as well as writing blog posts and articles that have featured in varied publications, and speaking at events all over the UK. She works with clients through her own consultancy, CP Data Protection, and also worked with Anthony Collins Solicitors for over 5 years, providing advice and training. Clients describe her as "friendly, professional and flexible", having a "warm and friendly approach" and her work as "excellent quality." Clare balances her work with family life, listening to rock music and podcasts (and making a true crime podcast too), and drinking too much coffee.

A Practical Guide to Data Protection in Social Housing

A Practical Guide to Data Protection in Social Housing

Clare Paterson

Law Brief Publishing

Published 2023 by Law Brief Publishing, an imprint of Law Brief Publishing Ltd
30 The Parks
Minehead
Somerset
TA24 8BT

www.lawbriefpublishing.com

Paperback: 978-1-916698-21-5

For Jie, Daniel and Beatrice.

PREFACE

I'm passionate about data protection, because at its core it's about protecting *people*.

The people I've met working in the social housing sector over the last 19 years are passionate about people too. And if we don't handle information about people with respect, how can we say we're treating the people themselves with respect?

If we want the people we work with and for to trust us, we must be able to let them know they can trust us with their precious personal data.

Keeping data safe and protected is so much more than storing it on a secure server or locked in a filing cabinet; it's about being clear why we want the data in the first place (and that reason being for a fair and lawful purpose!), being open and transparent, and only collecting, using, sharing and storing the *minimum* amount of data we *actually* need for those (fair and lawful!) purposes.

The very first Article of the GDPR itself explains that:

> *"This Regulation protects fundamental rights and freedoms of natural persons and in particular their right to the protection of personal data."*

Data protection rights are human rights, and I know that the people I work with care about human rights (I don't tend to work with clients that don't!)

If your work involves knowing *anything* whatsoever about your customers, tenants or colleagues, you're in the data world whether you realise it or not, and should be *protecting* that data too.

It shouldn't be a them-and-us situation though; we're all handling personal data, it's just some know a bit more about the data protection laws than others. So let's work together so that everyone handling data knows how to protect that data, and protect people.

The law quoted and information provided is believed to be accurate at 31st August 2023.

Clare Paterson
August 2023

CONTENTS

CHAPTER ONE

INTRODUCTION TO DATA PROTECTION IN SOCIAL HOUSING

Books and articles about data protection and the GDPR often feature images of computers and padlocks, sometimes a shield. These images represent the idea of keeping electronic data secure, which is of course crucial, but it is far from being the only important aspect of what we call 'data protection.'

Unfortunately, the term 'data protection' doesn't do itself justice, because it can sound like its focus is on keeping *data protected* from external leaks. However, there is much more to data protection law. Organisations also need to comply with the other aspects of data protection, which include considering the purpose for collecting the data in the first place, as well as accuracy, not keeping data for too long, and upholding individuals' rights, amongst other requirements.

The social housing sector exists to support people and communities, which means that social housing providers cannot operate without collecting, and using, a vast amount of information about the people they interact with; current, past, and potential tenants, customers, employees, and others.

There are undoubtedly many pros to having this data; being able to analyse tenant demographics, behaviour, and preferences can allow landlords to improve their services, and plan better for future needs and wants.

These benefits are often discussed in the housing sector, but the risks related to the collection and storage of personal data are not so widely acknowledged.

The benefits of data protection are not often examined either. The positive impacts of data protection compliance include increased trust and respect, better efficiency, improved tenant and employee relations, reduced costs, and reduced risks of causing people harm.

Data Protection Law

Data protection law is actually based on upholding human rights, and as such it holds so much potential for improving the lives of social housing tenants and employees, and society in general.

"This Regulation protects fundamental rights and freedoms of natural persons and in particular their right to the protection of personal data." [Art. 1 (UK)GDPR]

'Data Protection' includes more legal requirements than only the GDPR, too. In the UK we are subject to:

- The UK General Data Protection Regulation ('(UK)GDPR')
- The Data Protection Act 2018 ('DPA 2018')
- The Privacy and Electronic Communications Regulations (EC Directive) ('PECR')

There are also circumstances where social housing providers will need to consider the common law duty of confidentiality, and – less often – other laws relating to personal data such as the Access to Medical Reports Act.

Due to the nature of social housing, where organisations work with a huge number of individuals, a clear understanding of the scope of the legislation is critical.

"This Regulation does not apply to—

(a) the processing of personal data by an individual in the course of a purely personal or household activity;"

[Art. 2 (UK)GDPR]

When personal data is used for *"a purely personal or household activity"* the processing of that data is *not* subject to the (UK)GDPR, but that doesn't mean that customers or members of the public will never need to be aware of the law; see chapter 12 on the use of CCTV and ASB (Anti-social Behaviour).

Data Protection law does apply to most processing of personal data, relating to the people we interact with, our data subjects.

A 'data subject' is a person whose data is being processed, and 'process' means to do almost *anything* with or to that personal data.

In the social housing sector, we routinely process information about:

- Our colleagues, including employees, volunteers, board members;
- People who work with us, including colleagues from our contractors, our suppliers, Local Authorities, Regulators, Government departments, law enforcement, charities, community groups and more;
- People who live in our homes, including applicants and former tenants/customers;
- People who use our services, including potential and former customers;
- People linked to the people who live in our homes or use our services;

- People who make enquiries or complaints;

Myths about Data Protection

There are so many myths about data protection in general and about the GDPR and (UK)GDPR in particular. These range from needing consent to process any personal data, to the likelihood of being fined millions of pounds for any size of data breach, to organisations being prevented from helping vulnerable people due to the data protection laws. Unfortunately, these myths are often perpetuated by news articles and statements that are widely available.

To briefly address just those three myths, processing certainly *does not* always need consent, most organisations are *not* likely to be fined millions of pounds, and organisations including housing providers absolutely *can* help people in need without breaching data protection law. Each of these myths, and more, will be addressed throughout this book.

The Social Housing Sector's Values and Data Protection:

The social housing sector is largely based on values that are aligned with good data protection, even if it's not always recognised, perhaps due to the misunderstandings and myths around data protection.

Values including fairness, transparency, accountability, security, and respect for human rights can all be seen in the documented values, visions and missions of many social housing providers. What is not always realised is that they also all feature heavily in the data protection legislation.

It is unfortunate, but understandable, that many social housing providers will see data protection as a tick box exercise, or even as a blocker to achieving their goals. When in reality, the values in social housing align so closely with those that the data protection legislation is built upon.

CHAPTER TWO

DATA PROTECTION OFFICER ROLE & RESPONSIBILITIES

The overall responsibility for complying with data protection legislation lies with the legal entity, usually meaning the registered provider, *not* an individual. As with any legal requirements, employees are each responsible for complying with their employer's policies and procedures on the topic.

There are also a few circumstances where an individual *can* be guilty of committing a legal offence under the Data Protection Act 2018.

Chapter IV, Section 4 of the (UK)GDPR includes requirements for the role of "data protection officer", or DPO.

DPO is a specific role, with particular responsibilities, which are laid out in the (UK)GDPR. The criteria for assessing if an organisation is required to have a DPO are also included in the legislation.

Who needs a DPO?

Not all organisations are required to have an official DPO; whether or not an organisation *is* required to appoint a DPO is based on the nature of the data processing it carries out, unless it is a public authority or body; local authorities are *always* obliged to have a DPO.

Considering if other social housing providers require a DPO, the (UK)GDPR states that an organisation is required to have a DPO where its *"core activities consist of processing on a large scale of special categories... or personal data relating to criminal convictions and offences." [Article 37, (UK)GDPR]*

While it is generally accepted that social housing involves processing of special categories of personal data (see chapter 3) there is some discussion over whether it can be classed as being *"on a large scale."*

There is no clear definition of "large scale", but the ICO suggests that the relevant factors include: the number of data subjects, and the geographical spread of the data subjects and the processing, the amount of data being processed, and the range of data being processed, and how long the processing will continue.

However, whether or not a DPO is in post, the legal entity itself – the housing provider – has the same responsibility to comply with the data protection legislation, and in practice, social housing providers tend to appoint a DPO. Organisations choosing not to appoint a DPO should record their decision-making process for the sake of accountability, and any future challenge.

The DPO's responsibilities

The DPO's responsibilities are laid out in the (UK)GDPR, and the appointee should have the required abilities to undertake the role, including *"expert knowledge of data protection law and practices" [Article 37, (UK)GDPR].*

The legislation doesn't specify any particular qualifications, or length of experience, so housing providers appointing a DPO should consider carefully the combination of skills and experience required for the role.

The main purpose of the DPO role is two-fold;

- to advise the organisation and
- to monitor their compliance.

The DPO is not responsible for ensuring their employer always takes their advice, but are required to ensure they inform the organisation and its relevant employees of their legal obligations under the data protection legislation.

In particular, whenever their advice is requested with regards to a data protection impact assessment (DPIA), the DPO should provide that advice and monitor the progress of the DPIA (see chapter 9.)

The DPO's responsibility for monitoring includes monitoring the organisation's compliance with both the data protection legislation and the organisation's own data protection related policies.

The legislation specifies that those data protection related policies that will be monitored by the DPO should include "*the assignment of responsibilities, awareness-raising and training of staff involved in processing operations, and the related audits" [Art. 39 (UK)GDPR.]*

It's an important distinction, between the DPO's responsibilities in the DPO role and the organisation's responsibilities for complying with the legislation; the organisation is legally responsible for compliance, so should take care to appoint and support the DPO as appropriate. The responsibility for compliance cannot be delegated to the DPO or to any individual; it remains with the legal entity.

Another key duty of the DPO is to be contactable by the organisation's data subjects and to act as the liaison with the Information Commissioner's Office (ICO) as and when required.

Data Subjects should be able to contact the DPO so they can raise any queries about the processing of their data, including exercising their data rights (see chapter six). The DPO's contact details should be published to allow data subjects to contact them. In practice this is often a generic email address, such as dpo@organisation.com.

As with so much of the data protection legislation, undertaking the DPO role requires the risks to be assessed and taken into account. The (UK)GDPR highlights that, in the performance of their tasks, the DPO should "*have due regard*" to the risks connected with the data processing activities, "*taking into account the nature, scope, context and purposes of processing.*" [Art. 39 (UK)GDPR.]

Responsibilities towards the DPO

It is not just the DPO themselves with particular obligations related to the role, though; the organisation itself is required, by the (UK)GDPR, to ensure the DPO is able to carry out their role appropriately.

This means the housing provider is responsible for ensuring the following happens. The DPO should be:

- involved in anything in the organisation that relates to data protection, which in social housing is wide-reaching;

- able to access any and all of the data processing carried out by the organisation, so they can assess, advise on, and monitor all data processing, not just the processing that led to the appointment of a DPO i.e. the large-scale processing of special categories of personal data or criminal information;

- provided with the resources they need to carry out the DPO role appropriately;

- provided with the resources to maintain their data protection knowledge, including time and funding for training and learning materials;

- able to report directly, on data protection matters, to the highest level of management, usually the Board;

- bound by secrecy or confidentiality regarding their DPO duties and the information they are privy to in that role;

- *not* instructed on how to carry out the role of DPO (by the organisation); and
- *not* dismissed, or otherwise penalised, due solely to anything that relates to their carrying out of the DPO role in compliance with data protection legislation.

These last two points mean that the organisation should not interfere with the DPO's appropriate and lawful application of their own knowledge and expertise, and should not try to influence the outcome of any audit, data protection impact assessment, or similar.

This does not mean a DPO can never be dismissed or otherwise disciplined, though; the restriction only applies to wanting to silence or remove a DPO who is carrying out their role appropriately.

It can be assumed that this is included in the legislation due to the potential for conflict between organisations and the DPOs advising them about their data processing operations.

In smaller providers where a full-time DPO role is not deemed to be workable, one DPO can be appointed by a group of organisations, or the provider may contract with a consultant, or buy in a DPO as a service ('DPOaaS'), or a DPO can carry out other duties as part of their employment.

A DPO carrying out other duties is lawful so long as the other duties do not present a conflict of interests. In particular, duties that require the DPO to decide how and why the organisation will process personal data, for example as a head of HR, marketing, or customer service, would present a clear conflict.

Duties that don't present a conflict to the duties of a DPO of advising and monitoring, that may be undertaken in the social housing sector, include compiling responses to Subject Access Requests, and keeping the Records of Processing updated. Outside of data protection related tasks, duties could include supporting the governance or audit functions of the organisation. Making decisions about how and why personal data will be collected, processed, or used, must not be within the DPO's remit.

The DPO does not need to work alone in their role. Many housing providers have data protection teams, with colleagues who work on Subject Access Requests, breach investigations, Records of Processing, and more, while the DPO themselves holds the ultimate responsibility for both advising and monitoring the organisation's compliance, and DPOs often rely on external expertise and resources if needed.

The value of a DPO

DPOs can, and do, bring immense value to their employer, but it isn't always recognised. There is a common misconception in housing that data protection is more likely to stifle than support a landlord's objectives.

However, the use of personal data features in almost all areas of a landlord's work, and will have at least some impact on every department and team. As discussed in the introduction, the benefits of data protection compliance include increased trust and respect, better efficiency, improved tenant relations, and reduced risks of causing people harm.

Data, including personal data, can be as much of an asset to a housing provider as its properties, but it's easy for the DPO to be seen as a blocker to the organisation's objectives and aims. It doesn't have to be that way though.

It goes without saying that DPOs work hard to keep up to date with the prevailing and applicable legislation but there's something else DPOs tend to know. They often have a wealth of knowledge and insight about the organisations they work with.

This view of the whole picture – both the legal issues and the landlord's issues – can be put to excellent use to bring the law and the organisation together, instead of data protection being seen as something separate from the day-to-day operations.

In order to apply the requirements of data protection law to different departments or teams in a social housing provider, the DPO generally needs to understand the provider's drivers and objectives first. Also, as part of their work in advising their employer, DPOs often need to map out the processes and data flows in and around the organisation.

These aspects of their work give DPOs a holistic view of how things are actually happening. Coupled with their knowledge of the law, a DPO can help apply the law in a way that supports the organisations' strategic objectives. In fact, landlords will usually have the stated aims to be compliant with the law, and to operate in an efficient way. Embedding processes that support data protection will help both legal compliance and efficiency across the organisation.

There is also a growing emphasis on ESG (Environment, Social and Governance) in the social housing sector, and new initiatives in the name of ESG, as well as in the name of EDI (Equality/Equity, Diversity and Inclusion), often involve the collection and use of sensitive personal data, which gives DPOs another opportunity to add value and reduce risks to the business.

See chapter 13 on Insight & EDI work for more details.

Effective DPOs

The most effective way for DPOs to provide value is to be involved with any projects or new policies that involve processing of personal data as early as possible. Conflicts often arise between the organisation and the DPO when the DPO is not consulted before key decisions are made, such as what data will be collected, how it will be used, and which software will be procured. If these decisions are made without reference to data protection law, the DPO may have to advise that the plans are non-compliant, and recommend revisiting and unpicking them, which is usually costly in terms of time and money.

Having the DPO involved from the start, before any decisions are made, so key decisions can be made with reference to, and understanding of, the legal data protection requirements, can be referred to as 'privacy by design' or a personal phrase, 'baked-in data protection.'

To illustrate how this works, consider this question: Could you make some fruit scones, full of juicy raisins? The catch? You are presented with already-baked plain scones, and a bowl of raisins.

Being asked to use them to make some lovely fruit scones with the fruit evenly distributed through every bite is the same as the magic trick that DPOs are often asked to perform in their work.

The scones represent the landlord's processes and systems, the raisins represent compliance with data protection legislation, and the fruit scones are data protection compliant processes and systems.

The only way to get the raisins evenly spread through the scones is to start from scratch and bake them in, and it is exactly the same with data protection.

We need to 'bake-in' the consideration of data issues right from the planning stages whenever we're even thinking of introducing a new piece of software, project, or new way of working.

Tips for DPOs wanting to support their organisations to bake-in data protection in the social housing sector include using the language of the sector and of the organisation's objectives. For example, when working with resident-facing teams, focus on customers' experiences and common challenges they face, such as the current issues with damp and mould. When working with HR teams and managers, focus on employees' experience and values.

DPOs are sometimes seen as obstructive, but this is often because they're not involved in projects until the end, or almost the end; this leads to the DPO picking apart the project in an attempt to squeeze good data protection practices into it.

Thinking about data protection and getting DPOs involved from the earliest planning stages of projects, and new policies, is by far more efficient, and less stressful too.

It can seem like a DPO's work is never ending, and getting involved in more projects and policy updates may seem like an impossible task. It requires a move from 'fire-fighting' to a more strategic approach, and carving out time. Some ways a DPO can do this include referring colleagues to the data protection policy and guidance before they ask questions that will likely be answered by the documents, focussing on time management skills and having firm boundaries, and using what support is available from other professionals, in formal or informal arrangements.

CHAPTER THREE

PERSONAL DATA

The definition of personal data is wide-reaching, much wider than many people realise.

If an organisation can use a particular piece of data to identify an individual, either on its own or by adding it to data the organisation already holds, or could reasonably get hold of, that data is "personal data."

It can be likened to a jigsaw puzzle; if you have one piece and you can tell what the picture is from one piece, you have personal data. If you can't tell what the jigsaw's picture is from that one piece, but you are either in possession of, or can reasonably get hold of, another piece and the two pieces together would make the picture identifiable, that *first* puzzle piece *is* personal data, even if the second piece isn't immediately available.

Even information that has been inferred about an individual, either correctly or incorrectly, is regarded as personal data. In the jigsaw context, if you could *guess* what the picture is, from either one piece alone or with other pieces (that you have or could reasonably obtain), you have personal data, even if your guess is wrong.

All of this means that, to be personal data, information does *not* need to include a person's name, or even their initials. Other details can build a picture of that person, and tell us something about them, either factual data or inferred data.

For example, we may infer someone's race or ethnicity from their appearance or accent, we may deduce something about their health from seeing them using a walking aid, we may be able to work out someone's home address from photographs.

Even the opinions that a data subject holds are classed as their personal data, whether the opinions are based on fact or not. And, rather confusingly, opinions about a data subject, A, held by another individual, B, are A's personal data, but they are also B's personal data.

Conversely, while personal data does not need to include a name, not all instances of a person's own name will necessarily be regarded as personal data in all circumstances. See chapter 6 on data subjects' rights for more information on how this impacts data subject requests.

Generally speaking though, if data does, or could, identify an individual, it should be handled in compliance with all the requirements of data protection law.

In a social housing setting, it is more helpful to treat all information about people – whether it is about residents, colleagues, stakeholders, the public, or anyone else – with caution and care, because of the harm that can come to people if their information is shared when it shouldn't be, even if the leak doesn't actually come under data protection law.

For instance, information such as a name and phone number on a scrap of paper that's destined for the bin, rather than a file, might not be subject to the (UK)GDPR, strictly speaking. However, if it isn't disposed of carefully, it could be found by someone who chooses to misuse that data.

Likewise, verbal gossip between colleagues might not be subject to the (UK)GDPR either, but it can certainly cause harm.

Both these circumstances are more about confidentiality than the (UK)GDPR or related legislation. A breach of confidentiality would likely be a breach of employment contract terms though or could constitute misconduct.

Examples of personal data held by social housing providers, about their tenants, customers, employees, stakeholders, and other data subjects include the following, some of which are more obviously 'personal data' than others:

- name
- address
- contact details
- employee reference number
- customer account number
- opinions *about* the data subject
- opinions *held by* the data subject (about anything)
- employment history
- criminal record
- family information
- marital status
- financial information
- information produced during interactions with the data subject or other people
- health or disability information
- race or ethnic origin

- religious beliefs
- sexual orientation

The last four items in this list are types of data that are defined as 'Special Categories of Personal Data.'

Special Categories of Personal Data

A subset of personal data is designated, in the legislation, as special categories of personal data, listed in Article 9 in the (UK)GDPR:

- Race or ethnic origin
- Health data, both physical and mental health
- Sexual orientation, or data concerning a person's sex life
- Religious or philosophical beliefs
- Political opinions
- Trade union membership
- Biometric data, when used to identify an individual
- Genetic data

Other data, such as financial details, may be regarded as sensitive, but is not included in the legal definition 'special categories.' See the section below for how criminal information is classed.

Social housing providers collect many types of special categories of personal data, for a variety of reasons related to allocating and managing tenancies, most often health and disability data. For reasons linked to

Equality, Diversity, and Equality (EDI), housing providers sometimes also gather information about their colleagues' and tenants' ethnicity, sexual orientation, and religious beliefs. Health and disability data is also gathered for EDI reasons.

In chapter 5 we look in more detail at the purposes for which social housing providers collect and use special categories of personal data.

The (UK)GDPR requires that special categories of personal data are handled with a higher level of control than most other personal data, largely due to the fact that people are often discriminated against, and suffer negative treatment, because of their characteristics that come under the heading of special categories of personal data.

In chapter 5 we will look at the higher barriers to lawfully processing this type of data in more detail.

Criminal information

Any information relating to a person's criminal charges, prosecutions, or even alleged criminal activity, is "criminal information" under the legislation.

The (UK)GDPR requires this data to be treated with a higher level of control, in a similar way to special categories of personal data.

Social housing providers often collect and hold different types of criminal information, for a variety of purposes related to allocating homes and managing tenancies. In chapter 5 we will look in more detail at the purposes and legal requirements for handling this data.

Anonymous data

Anonymous data is not subject to the data protection legislation, but it can be very complex to make personal data truly anonymous. This is because of the wide-reaching definition of personal data, that a piece of information is considered personal data even if it needs another piece of information added to it, in order to identify an individual.

The more pieces of information that are together in one place or held by the same organisation, like in the jigsaw puzzle example, the more likely it is an induvial is identifiable from the information.

For example, just knowing a person's age, gender and the team they work in could identify an individual colleague. Or a person's postcode, job, and information about their disability could identify an individual resident.

It may not always be necessary to make personal data fully anonymous in order to process it lawfully for internal reporting and modelling purposes. However, when data is being shared externally for case studies and similar, it's often necessary to make it truly anonymous first. This is the case if there is no lawful basis to rely on when sharing or publishing the data.

Therefore, strict protocols should be followed in order to ensure data is truly anonymised before it is shared. This can include stripping out, or even changing, any and all identifying characteristics of the person, or aggregating several people's data in a way that prohibits identification of an individual.

CHAPTER FOUR

THE (UK)GDPR PRINCIPLES

A common misconception about data protection is that it is focussed on protecting data, through cyber security measures. This is an understandable misconception, as that is exactly what the phrase 'data protection' sounds like it means.

However, the (UK)GDPR is a principles-based law, and security is just one of the principles. The key word in the principles is "purpose", as we need to understand the purpose for the data processing before considering how to comply with the principles, including the security principle.

Being principles-based means there are very few straightforward rules, where the requirements are black and white. Instead, words like "appropriate" feature often in the legislation, meaning organisations need to consider the risks and potential outcomes of each case of data processing. We will look at assessing the risks in more detail in chapter 9.

The first six principles of the (UK)GDPR relate to how, and for what purpose, the personal data is processed. They are included in full below for reference, but to summarise:

The (UK)GDPR requires that personal data shall be:

- processed only on a lawful basis, processed fairly, and the processing should be transparent to data subjects;

- collected for specific purposes (which are lawful, fair and transparent), and used only for those purposes in most circumstances;

- adequate and relevant to the purposes for which it was collected and is being used;

- accurate and up to date as necessary for its purposes;

- kept (in a format that allows individuals to be identifiable) only for as long as is necessary for its original purposes, plus any compatible (and lawful) purposes; and

- processed and kept securely.

The seventh principle, known as 'the Accountability principle', requires organisations to be able to demonstrate that they are complying with the other requirements of the (UK)GDPR.

> *Personal data shall be:*
>
> *(a) processed lawfully, fairly and in a transparent manner in relation to the data subject ('lawfulness, fairness and transparency');*
>
> *(b) collected for specified, explicit and legitimate purposes and not further processed in a manner that is incompatible with those purposes; further processing for archiving purposes in the public interest, scientific or historical research purposes or statistical purposes shall, in accordance with Article 89(1), not be considered to be incompatible with the initial purposes ('purpose limitation');*
>
> *(c) adequate, relevant and limited to what is necessary in relation to the purposes for which they are processed ('data minimisation');*
>
> *(d) accurate and, where necessary, kept up to date; every reasonable step must be taken to ensure that personal data that are inaccurate,*

having regard to the purposes for which they are processed, are erased or rectified without delay ('accuracy');

(e) kept in a form which permits identification of data subjects for no longer than is necessary for the purposes for which the personal data are processed; personal data may be stored for longer periods insofar as the personal data will be processed solely for archiving purposes in the public interest, scientific or historical research purposes or statistical purposes in accordance with Article 89(1) subject to implementation of the appropriate technical and organisational measures required by this Regulation in order to safeguard the rights and freedoms of the data subject ('storage limitation');

(f) processed in a manner that ensures appropriate security of the personal data, including protection against unauthorised or unlawful processing and against accidental loss, destruction or damage, using appropriate technical or organisational measures ('integrity and confidentiality').

[Art. 5 (UK)GDPR]

Complying with the rest of the first six principles often relies on getting the first principle right in the first place; if a landlord is processing personal data without a fair and lawful basis (as required by the first principle), the landlord can never comply with the principles of purpose limitation, data minimisation, accuracy, or storage limitation.

This is because these principles require the data to be handled appropriately according to the processing purpose. So without understanding what the lawful purpose is for the processing, we can't decide how much data we need, or how long to keep it, and so on.

If there is *no* lawful purpose, everything else we do with that data is unlawful, even if the data is kept securely.

Once the first principle has been addressed, the next five principles can be addressed, and these all have one thing in common; they can all be linked to the need to reduce various things.

We should seek to reduce the amount of data collected, held, stored, accessed, used, analysed, and shared, as well as reducing the amount of time it's kept for. Putting in place appropriate security measures should reduce the chances of the data being lost or misused.

Data can be attractive, due to its potential for gaining insights, and housing providers can find it tempting, which can lead to an approach of wanting more and more. In this way, data can be compared to popcorn; an overflowing large bucket of popcorn is tempting, but in reality it is hard to control too much popcorn and it can quickly get very messy.

Reducing the amount of popcorn in the bucket to a manageable amount, makes it much easier to control it, and reduce the risk of any nasty accidents. It is the same with data; the more we collect, the higher the likelihood of causing harm to both the data subjects and the organisation.

Fair, Lawful & Transparent Processing

The first principle, that personal data shall be processed in a manner that is fair, lawful and transparent, acts as a jumping off point for the next five principles.

It relates to the purpose for which the organisation is processing the data – that is, doing almost anything with it – in the first place. Without a lawful and fair purpose to be collecting, using, sharing, analysing, etc. that data, you have an uphill battle to comply with any of the other principles.

We can divide the first principle into three separate parts:

- Fair

- Lawful
- And transparent

Fair is a subjective term but generally is understood to mean what a reasonable person and society at large would expect. Assessing fairness means considering not only the individual's expectations and desires, but the public in general. For example, a parolee might not want their parole officer to process information about them breaching their parole conditions, but it is in the public interest for the parole officer to do so.

Lawful is much easier to pin down, especially when we read further on in the legislation; see chapter 5 for the detail of how to ensure processing is lawful.

Transparency means making sure that the people whose data is being processed are aware of it, usually achieved by the organisation making it completely transparent. Meaning that information about the data processing is freely available, where people would expect it to be made available, and the processing itself, and the reasons behind it, are not being hidden.

People don't need to, and should not be asked to, sign or tick to say they *accept* a privacy notice; it is an information notice, not a contract.

Sometimes it seems that organisations are more comfortable getting their data subjects to say they agree to the Privacy Notice, but it doesn't have any legal effect and it is possible it would just cause confusion.

There are a limited number of exemptions to the transparency requirement, which are laid down in Schedule 2 of the DPA 2018. They are largely, but not exactly, the same exemptions that may be applied to the right of access, and include where data is being processed for the purposes of crime and taxation, a number of listed *"functions designed to protect the public"*, *"journalistic, academic, artistic and literary purposes"*, and management forecasts amongst other purposes, so long as complying with the transparency requirements would likely prejudice the purposes of the processing.

In general though, if a social housing provider is reluctant to reveal any of its routine data processing, because of a fear that data subjects would not be happy, that is a clear red flag and a firm reason to investigate the fairness and lawfulness of that processing.

Privacy Notices

When personal data is collected directly from a data subject, the law requires that the data controller provides the person with certain details about the processing. This is usually presented in the form of an online Privacy Notice but should be layered where possible. The full Privacy Notice should be at least signposted to at the time of the data collection, and a short explanation for the data collection should be provided on the form or other data-collection method itself.

Privacy Notice information must include, as laid down in the (UK)GDPR:

a. the identity and contact details of the organisation and contact details of the Data Protection Officer (or the data protection lead, in the absence of an officially designated DPO);

b. the reasons for which the organisation is processing personal data, and each lawful basis for the processing;

c. where the lawful basis is 'legitimate interests', an explanation of those legitimate interests;

d. if the data is needed for a contract or for a statutory requirement, an explanation of the possible consequences of failing to provide it;

e. any automated data processing and decision making where the outcome could have a significant effect on an individual (including profiling), and its possible consequences;

f. who the data will be shared with, or the types of organisations/people the data will be shared with;

g. if the data will be stored or transferred data outside of the UK, the fact that this will happen, and the safeguards that are in place;

h. how long the data will be stored, or how decisions are made about how long the data will be kept in an identifiable format;

i. the legal rights that data subjects have, and the right to object to processing should be highlighted;

j. the data subjects' right to withdraw consent at any time, if consent is the lawful basis being relied on for the processing; and

k. the data subjects' right to complain about the processing of their data to the relevant supervisory authority, the Information Commissioner's Office in the UK.

When personal data is collected via a third party, the organisation is also required to inform the data subjects about:

a. the categories of personal data concerned; and

b. the source of the personal data.

The information in Privacy Notices must be made available to data subjects in writing no later than one month after the organisation receives the data, unless a legal exemption applies, as above. If the data is being used to contact an individual, and it is within the one-month timescale, the Privacy Notice information should be provided at the time of contact.

Purpose Limitation

This principle requires that personal data is processed only for purposes that have a lawful basis, and which are transparent. In most circumstances it also means the purposes should be the purposes for which the data was originally collected, but it can be extended to include processing for "compatible purposes".

To assess whether any new planned purpose is a compatible process, the organisation must consider, amongst other things, the context in which the data was collected, what the data subject would reasonably expect to be done with their data, the link between the original processing purpose and the proposed new purpose, and the related risks.

Assessing the risks includes considering the nature of the data, the possible consequences of the new processing, the potential for those consequences to come about from the new processing, and any appropriate safeguards against the risks, that are either already in place or should be put into place. (See chapter 9 for more details on assessing the risks of new processing.)

It is not as simple as saying, for example, that a new purpose for processing data that relates to a tenancy will always be a 'compatible purpose' because it is linked to the provision of homes and tenancies. Each new purpose should be carefully assessed, and the other principles complied with too, with regards to that new purpose, including being transparent about it, and deciding how long the data needs to be retained, and so on.

Social housing providers sometimes collect personal data for reporting purposes, such as for CORE (COntinuous REcording of Lettings and Sales in Social Housing in England). Landlords should distinguish between data that is collected for CORE reporting purposes, and data collected for internal purposes; data cannot automatically be recorded and used by a housing provider for its own purposes because it's collected for CORE. The organisation must ensure it has its own lawful basis for collecting the data for its own use, as well as complying with the other principles, if it plans to keep the data for its own use.

Data Minimisation

To meet the requirement for data minimisation, data collection systems and forms – both hard copy and electronic – must be carefully designed to collect only the personal data that is required for the processing purpose in question.

This highlights the importance of the organisation having a clear understanding of its own processes and objectives, in order to really understand what data is necessary and what is additional. Only data that is necessary for a lawful purpose should be collected, and personal data must not be collected 'just in case.'

Once data is held by the organisation, processes should be designed as much as reasonably possible to ensure that no one views, handles or otherwise processes data that is not required as part of their role.

Employees are responsible for not misusing any data they come into contact with as part of their role, or in error, and doing so could mean the employee is guilty of committing an offence under the DPA 2018. The employer though, is responsible for putting controls into place to reduce the likelihood that people will come across data they don't need to have access to, or that they will be easily able to misuse data they come across or use in their role.

One major way that personal data is collected by housing providers is during the application process, both customer applications and employee applications.

Therefore, landlords should review their application process on a regular basis to ensure there is a robust lawful basis for the purposes for which each type of personal data being collected is being used.

Data Accuracy

The requirement to ensure personal data is accurate and up to date is risk-based; the higher the risk of harm to the data subjects by their data being inaccurate or out of date, the more emphasis should be put on processes to keep the data accurate and up to date.

In the social housing sector, an inaccurate date of birth for a child could affect an allocation, where the number of bedrooms a family is eligible for is based on the ages of their children. On the other hand, an inaccurate date of birth for an adult tenant may have little to no effect much of the time.

Data Retention

People often ask how many years the data protection legislation allows organisations to keep personal data, but there are no requirements in the (UK)GDPR, DPA2018 or PECR, for retention to be a particular length of time.

How long personal data is retained should be based on the original purpose for which the data was processed, but it is also valid to increase the retention period if the data is now being processed for an additional (fair, lawful and transparent) purpose with a longer retention period.

Retention periods are based on the specific requirements of the purposes for processing, and are based on laws outside of data protection, such as tax and health and safety, as well as official guidance or good practice in the housing sector.

The National Housing Federation has guidance, and an example retention schedule,

The National Housing Federation has guidance, and an example retention schedule, available on its website, as a starting point for landlords creating their own retention policies and schedules.

Producing the schedule is just the start, though; ensuring data can and will be deleted or destroyed when it comes to the end of its retention period is often a challenge. If possible, it is ideal to build in retention and deletion rules to new software at the very beginning of its set-up.

Data Security

As discussed earlier, 'data security' is often thought of as being a synonym for 'data protection' or as being the focus of data protection. It is of course a crucial element of data protection, and most of the cases in the headlines and any GDPR cases that attract monetary penalties tend to be regarding a breach of data security.

We are used to hearing about cyber-attacks and data breaches in all sectors, and the social housing sector is not spared. Housing providers of all sizes can be, and have been, casualties, suffering data loss, ransomware attacks, financial loss, and have had to close their systems down to assess a situation or to prevent further damage.

The effects of a data breach can be significant. If data is obtained by someone with ill intentions, the data subjects – tenants, customers, employees, and anyone else whose data is obtained – can experience identity fraud, financial loss, anxiety, significant inconvenience, harassment, and even physical harm if details about one or more vulnerable people is accessed by someone intending to hurt them.

Not all vulnerabilities are obvious, or known to the landlord, and each person's individual circumstances can impact the risk represented by a particular category of data. For many people, their name and address may represent only a low risk if it was obtained by a hacker. For a survivor of domestic abuse however, or an adoptive family, their name and address falling into the hands of unknown people, and potentially into the hands of their abuser or biological relatives, could represent a huge risk to their wellbeing. Sadly, these are not just made-up examples, and these events have occurred.

Even when data isn't accessed by an external party, a cyber-attack can still hold up normal activities in the organisation, keeping operations at a standstill for weeks or even months.

Consider how reliant housing providers, and their partners such as repairs providers and local authorities, are on electronic systems, software and data. Organisations face being unable to provide their services if the systems or data are held to ransom, deleted, or if access is closed down by the organisation itself until able to return to normal operations in a safe manner.

Although organisations are required to decide what measures are appropriate, Article 32 of the (UK)GDPR does build on the data security principle by stating that security measures shall include *"as appropriate:*

> *(a) the pseudonymisation and encryption of personal data;*
>
> *(b) the ability to ensure the ongoing confidentiality, integrity, availability and resilience of processing systems and services;*
>
> *(c) the ability to restore the availability and access to personal data in a timely manner in the event of a physical or technical incident;*
>
> *(d) a process for regularly testing, assessing and evaluating the effectiveness of technical and organisational measures for ensuring the security of the processing.*

As with much of data protection, the measures should be risk-based and also reflect what is possible. When deciding what is "appropriate" controllers must *take "into account the state of the art, the costs of implementation and the nature, scope, context and purposes of processing as well as the risk of varying likelihood and severity for the rights and freedoms of natural persons." [Art. 32 (UK)GDPR]*

See chapter 10 for more details on data security and breaches.

Accountability

The final principle, the seventh, is accountability, which requires organisations to be able to demonstrate that they are complying with the (UK)GDPR:

> *"The controller shall be responsible for, and be able to demonstrate compliance with, paragraph 1 ('accountability')."*
>
> *[Art. 5.2 (UK)GDPR]*

The (UK)GDPR includes some specific requirements for organisations to demonstrate their accountability, including:

- implementing 'data protection by design and default' where applicable,
- carrying out DPIAs (data protection impact assessments) when required (see chapter 9 for details),
- appointing a DPO (data protection officer) if required (see chapter 2 for details), and
- having particular documentation in place;
    - RoP (records of processing),
    - appropriate contracts in place with data processors (see chapter 8 for details), and
    - general documents that support compliance, such as policies and procedures.

Many organisations, including housing providers, are also required to register with the ICO and pay the registration fee.

The ICO (Information Commissioner's Office) has created an Accountability Framework and self-assessment tool which can be accessed on its website, that organisations can use to measure their accountability measures and highlight areas for improvement.

There is no one-size-fits-all solution for demonstrating accountability, and like so much in data protection, each organisation's measures should be proportionate to the risks.

Data Protection by Design and by Default

Implementing 'data protection by design and default', which is in Art. 25 (UK)GDPR, requires an approach across the organisation that acknowledges that data processing cannot be easily separated out from the day-to-day business of providing social housing; data processing risks *are* business risks.

This is of course, easier said than done, and cannot be done alone. Chapter 9 provides details of how to carry out DPIAs, as well as when a DPIA is required in social housing settings.

To fully implement data protection by design and default, though, takes more than DPIAs alone; it takes support and understanding from all colleagues, including all levels of management and the board.

> The ideal state, of always considering data protection by design and by default, involves the organisation putting in place *"appropriate technical and organisational measures... which are designed to implement data-protection principles...in an effective manner"* and integrating *"the necessary safeguards into the processing in order to meet the requirements of this Regulation and protect the rights of data subjects."*
>
> *[Art.25 (UK)GDPR]*

The right stage of a project, or new way of working, to implement these measures and integrate these safeguards is – as laid down in Article 25 – "*both at the time of the determination of the means for processing and at the time of the processing itself*".

Which means, in practice, that consideration of all the potential data protection compliance issues and potential impacts on the rights of data subjects must be undertaken right at the start of any project or new way of working that involves the processing of personal data.

The more awareness that the organisation, its employees, and the housing sector in general, have about the (wide-reaching) definitions of both 'personal data' and 'processing', the better chance there is for achieving data protection by design and default.

RoP (records of processing)

All organisations that either have 250 or more employees, or process special categories of personal data or criminal information, are required to produce and maintain a Record of Processing, or RoP.

Special categories personal data includes information about a person's race or ethnic origin, health, sexual orientation or sex life, religious or philosophical beliefs, political opinions, or trade union membership, as well as biometric data that is being used to identify an individual, and genetic data.

Social Housing providers will usually process at least some special categories of data or criminal information – whether relating to its residents or employees – so will be required to keep a RoP, even with fewer than 250 employees.

Under Art. 30 of the (UK)GDPR, housing providers acting as data controllers are required to include the following information in their RoP:

- Organisation name and contact details;
- The DPO's (data protection officer) name and contact details if one has been appointed (see chapter 2 on DPOs);
- Name and contact details of any joint controllers (see chapter 8 for more information on controllers and processors);
- The purposes of the data processing undertaken by the organisation;
- The categories of data subjects, whose data is processed by the organisation;
- The categories of personal data being processed;
- The categories of organisations the data is shared with;
- Name of any third countries (or international organisations) outside of the UK that data is transferred to as part of an international data transfer;
- Where possible, the retention timescales for each category of personal data being processed; and
- Where possible, a general description of the organisation's technical and organisational security measures around personal data and its processing.

Most housing providers will be a data controller, but some may be a data processor in some circumstances. See chapter 8 for more information on controllers and processors.

Data processors, that are obliged to keep a RoP, must record the following items:

- Organisation name and contact details;
- The DPO's (data protection officer) name and contact details if one has been appointed (see chapter 2 on DPOs);
- Name and contact details (including their DPO) of all the controllers on whose behalf the processor carries out processing;
- The categories of data processing carried out on behalf of each controller;
- Name of any third countries (or international organisations) outside of the UK that data is transferred to as part of an international data transfer;
- Where possible, a general description of the organisation's technical and organisational security measures around personal data and its processing.

In practice, there are a multitude of ways to create a RoP, from simple spreadsheets to complex databases built on specialised software, and the most appropriate should be chosen by each organisation, based on requirements and resources.

It is very easy for a RoP and the work involved in creating and maintaining it to be seen as a drain on resources, as bureaucracy and red-tape with no real benefit. And it certainly can become this!

There is no set format for a RoP, so ideally it should be created in a format that serves the organisation best. At the time of writing, the ICO's online guidance recommends starting by mapping out the data flows in and across the organisation, to give a clear picture of the data that is being processed and the data subjects involved, as well as where, how, and why data is being processed. Mapping data flows is always a valuable exercise.

From the data maps, a RoP can be formed as either one document or many, most often based on each business function. Adding other information to the RoP can be useful. For example, adding information about the lawful bases being relied on for each type of processing will help when it comes to maintaining Privacy Notices.

In addition, when special categories of personal data are being processed on the lawful basis of either 'Employment, Social Protection or Social Security Law' or 'Substantial Public Interest' (with a few exceptions), the DPA 2018 requires that the RoP include some extra information.

If criminal information is being processed on the basis of either 'Substantial Public Interest' (with a few exceptions) or the 'Additional Conditions' in Part 3 of Schedule 1 of the DPA 2018 requires that the RoP include the same extra information.

The extra information to be added to the RoP in relation to these types of processing, is:

- which condition (from Schedule 1 of the DPA2018) is relied on for the particular processing purpose,
- what lawful basis from Article 6 of the (UK)GDPR is relied upon for the processing, and
- whether the personal data being processed is retained and then deleted or destroyed in accordance with the 'appropriate policy document(s) that are a requirement of relying on most of the conditions in Schedule 1 of the DPA2018, and, if not, the reasons for not following those policies.

A RoP doesn't necessarily need to be created from scratch; if the organisation already maintains other records that include some of the required information, they can be referred or linked to. Ideally, a RoP should support the organisation to manage personal data lawfully, not be solely an administrative burden.

Policies and procedures

To demonstrate compliance with the (UK)GDPR, Recital 78 states that *"the controller should adopt internal policies and implement measures which meet in particular the principles of data protection by design and data protection by default."*

Another reference to *"data protection by design and by default"* there, and the key phrase there is *"and implement measures"*, because written policies are of course almost useless on their own; appropriate controls and procedures should be in place to ensure the policies are followed. And again, appropriateness should be decided by the organisation, based on the risks posed by the data processing in question.

Approved Codes of Conduct

Another way of demonstrating compliance with the (UK)GDPR, at least in part, is proof of adhering to a relevant code of conduct. At the time of writing, there are no approved codes of conduct available, although a social housing code of conduct is in progress. Approval must then come from the ICO.

ICO registration and fee

Under the 'Data Protection (Charges and Information) Regulations 2018', data controllers are required to pay a registration fee to the ICO unless their type of data processing is exempt. Exempt processing relates mostly to individuals acting in a personal capacity, charities or not-for-profits whose processing only involves providing a service to its members, processing that is confined to the administration of colleagues, or processing that is confined to financial issues and finance and management planning, including working with customers, and deciding whether or not to take on a particular customer (but not if data is obtained from a credit reference agency.)

Due to the nature of social housing work, which often involves working with the wider community, in partnerships, and sometimes carrying out analysis and research, social housing providers are unlikely to be exempt from paying the fee.

The fee is currently arranged into three tiers:

Tier 1 includes 'micro-organisations' that have 10 or fewer members of staff, or an annual turnover of £632,000 or less, or are a charity. The annual tier 1 fee is currently £40.

Tier 2 includes 'small and medium organisations' that don't fall into tier 1 but have 250 or fewer members of staff, or an annual turnover of £36million or less. The annual tier 2 fee is currently £60.

Tier 3 is for all other organisations who are neither exempt from the fee nor in tiers 1 or 2. The annual tier 3 fee is currently £2,900.

VAT is not payable on the fee, and the ICO currently offers a small discount on payments made by direct debit.

Many, but not all, social landlords will have charitable status or what is known as 'exempt charitable status', putting them in tier 1, regardless of size. For example, a registered society within the meaning of the Co-operative and Community Benefit Societies Act 2014 that is also a non-profit registered provider of social housing (or is also registered in the register of social landlords in Wales) has 'exempt charitable status' under the Charities Act 2011.

In a group structure, however, it is important to note that each legal entity needs its own registration and to pay its own fee, and some housing groups contain profit-making entities.

Failure to pay the relevant fee can result in being fined by the ICO, up to around £4,000.

CHAPTER FIVE

LAWFUL BASES FOR DATA PROCESSING

As discussed earlier, the first principle should be addressed first, and the key part of that is identifying the lawful basis/purpose of the data processing. Identifying the purpose and matching it to a valid lawful basis is like a hurdle, which you need to get over before you can do anything else.

The lawful bases are listed in Article 6 of the (UK)GDPR. Consent is listed first in the legislation, but this time, it's not helpful to be in that order; in practice, consent should be the last resort.

> *1. Processing shall be lawful only if and to the extent that at least one of the following applies:*
>
> *(a) the data subject has given consent to the processing of his or her personal data for one or more specific purposes;*
>
> *(b) processing is necessary for the performance of a contract to which the data subject is party or in order to take steps at the request of the data subject prior to entering into a contract;*
>
> *(c) processing is necessary for compliance with a legal obligation to which the controller is subject;*
>
> *(d) processing is necessary in order to protect the vital interests of the data subject or of another natural person;*
>
> *(e) processing is necessary for the performance of a task carried out in the public interest or in the exercise of official authority vested in the controller;*

(f) processing is necessary for the purposes of the legitimate interests pursued by the controller or by a third party, except where such interests are overridden by the interests or fundamental rights and freedoms of the data subject which require protection of personal data, in particular where the data subject is a child.

Point (f) of the first subparagraph shall not apply to processing carried out by public authorities in the performance of their tasks.

[Art. 6 (UK)GDPR]

Instead of looking at the lawful bases in the order they appear in the legislation, when considering the appropriate lawful basis, the list is more useful this way around:

- Necessary for a contract with the data subject
- Necessary for compliance with a legal obligation
- Necessary to protect vital interests
- Necessary for the performance of a task in the public interest
- Necessary for the legitimate interests of the controller or 3rd party (although public authorities cannot usually rely on this basis)
- And finally, only if nothing else applies, the consent of the data subject.

Necessary for contract

This lawful basis only applies if the data subject is subject to the contract, and the processing is necessary for the purposes of the contract, or is necessary to take actions in order to enter into the contract.

In the main, social housing providers process the personal data of their tenants and customers on the lawful basis of contract; the processing is necessary for the purposes of the tenancy agreement, including assessing an application for housing.

And for employees, much of the data processing will be necessary for the employment contracts, including the application stage.

Both tenancy agreements and employment contracts are legal contracts for the purposes of relying on the lawful basis of *"necessary for contract"*.

"Necessary" is a high bar to reach, though. Adding unnecessary, nice-to-have, requirements to a tenancy agreement or employment contract will *not* be covered by that lawful basis.

The key word in all the lawful bases in Article 6 is "necessary."

Necessary for a legal obligation

This lawful basis applies if the processing is necessary for the controller to be able to comply with a legal obligation it is subject to. In social housing, it is crucial that landlords are aware of the delineation between processing they are legally obliged to carry out, and processing that is optional.

It is not uncommon for social housing providers or its employees to believe they are under a legal obligation to collect certain data for a particular purpose when they are not; this occurs when best-practice recommendations are mistaken for legal requirements, or when legal requirements are mistakenly translated into a request for personal data.

For example, the Equality Act requires that organisations don't discriminate against people based on their characteristics. This is often understood as there being a legal obligation to collect information about people's characteristics, but that is not necessarily the case. See chapter 13 for more details on EDI data collection.

Necessary to protect vital interests

This lawful basis applies if the processing is necessary to protect the "vital interests" of any person – the data subject themselves or any other individual. Protecting vital interests is described in Recital 46 as:

> *"an interest which is essential for the life of the data subject or that of another... person".* The recital goes on to clarify that *"Some types of processing may serve both important grounds of public interest and the vital interests of the data subject...including for monitoring epidemics and their spread or in... humanitarian emergencies, in particular in...natural and man-made disasters."*

The bar is set high, therefore, for processing to be necessary for protecting vital interests; it is often described as a matter of life and death.

Necessary for a task in the public interest

This lawful basis applies if the processing is necessary for the controller to be able to carry out a task that is in the public interest, or is necessary for the controller to carry out its official functions. In both cases, the task or function, must have a clear basis in domestic UK law to be valid. This lawful basis is used in the main by public authorities, that have official functions bestowed by the law.

Legitimate Interests

If none of the other lawful bases are appropriate, the controller can consider if the processing is necessary for the purposes of its own legitimate interests, or the legitimate interests of another organisation. It will only apply, however, if the interests are not overridden by the interests, rights, and freedoms of the data subjects.

To make this judgement, a Legitimate Interests Assessment is required, under the legislation, to be carried out and documented, before relying on Legitimate Interests a the lawful basis for the processing:

There are three parts to a Legitimate Interests Assessment:

- What is the outcome the processing will achieve, and how important is that outcome?
- Is this processing the only way to achieve that outcome?
- Finally, weigh the legitimate interest of achieving that outcome against the interests, rights, and freedoms of the data subjects.

If the interests, rights and freedoms of the data subjects would be unfairly impacted by the processing, the lawful basis does not apply.

The Assessment can be documented separately or built into the controller's Record of Processing document or system. And a summary of the decision must be included in the Privacy Notice, where lawful bases are explained.

Public authorities cannot rely on Legitimate Interests as a lawful basis for processing related to their official functions and tasks carried out in the public interest, but they can rely on it for processing for other purposes, which are outside of their official functions and tasks.

Consent

As above, consent should usually be the last resort, but there are two situations where consent is *always* the *only* available lawful basis.

Consent is required for setting non-essential website cookies and for sending direct unsolicited electronic marketing (e.g. emails and SMS messages) to individuals.

Under the PECR (Privacy and Electronic Communications Regulations), non-essential website cookies must only be placed on a website visitor's device with their freely-given consent, which allows visitors to consent or decline non-essential cookies.

Consent is not required for essential cookies, but cookies are only classed as 'essential' if they are necessary to make the website work properly for the visitor, and the way the visitor would want the website to work. Meaning that analytics cookies wouldn't be classed as essential cookies, as these are for the benefit of the website owner, not the visitor.

For more information on sending direct marketing, see chapter 14 on contacting people.

Relying on consent when another lawful basis would be more appropriate can make things awkward and confusing for both the controller and the data subjects. Consider what would happen if the processing was based on consent and the data subject withdrew their consent (Article 7 of the (UK)GDPR states that "*It shall be as easy to withdraw as to give consent.*") If another lawful basis could take the place of that consent, then consent isn't likely to be the correct lawful basis in the first place.

To be valid, Article 7 of the (UK)GDPR states that any request for consent must be *"clearly distinguishable from... other matters, in an intelligible and easily accessible form, using clear and plain language"* and any declaration of consent that breaches this requirement will *not* be binding consent. Consent must be freely-given too, and the controller must be able to demonstrate that consent has been provided by the data subject.

Because consent must be freely-given, it is unlikely that consent will be an appropriate lawful basis for processing carried out by an individual's landlord or their employer, because of the in-built imbalance of power in the dynamics between the data subject and the controller.

Lawful basis for Special categories of personal data

If the data being processed is, or includes, special categories of personal data (race/ethnicity, religious/philosophical beliefs, political beliefs, health/disability, sexuality/sexual life, biometric data used for identification, genetic data, or trade union membership) there are *two* hurdles to get over for the processing to be lawful.

As well as meeting a lawful basis from the lists in Article 6, another basis (or strictly speaking an exemption) must apply in order to make the processing lawful.

These are listed in Article 9 of the (UK)GDPR and include:

- the processing is necessary for carrying out the controller's legal obligations, or allowing anyone to exercise their legal rights, but only if those obligations or rights are under employment law, or social security law, or social protection law;

- the processing is necessary for safeguarding the vital interests of an individual and the data subject is incapable of giving consent (e.g. in emergency, life or death situations);

- the processing is necessary for pursuing or defending legal claims or where the courts are acting in their judicial capacity;

- the processing relates to personal data manifestly made public by the data subject themselves;

- the processing is necessary for the purposes of preventive or occupational health/medicine, or health care, but only where the data is processed by or under the supervision of a medical professional;

- the processing is necessary in the interests of public health, on the basis of law;

- the processing is necessary for archiving purposes in the public interest, scientific or historical research purposes, or statistical purposes based in law; or

- the processing is necessary for the substantial public interest, for purposes with a basis in law, specifically the DPA 2018 (see details below).

If none of these (or the other Article 9 lawful bases) apply, the processing will be lawful only if the data subject has given their *explicit*, clear, specific, freely-given consent.

One other lawful basis is listed in Article 9, but the ones above are those most likely to apply in social housing.

For completeness, the other available Article 9 lawful basis applies to charities, clubs, and groups with "*a political, philosophical, religious or trade union aim*" as follows:

> *"(d) processing is carried out in the course of its legitimate activities with appropriate safeguards by a foundation, association or any other not-for-profit body with a political, philosophical, religious or trade union aim and on condition that the processing relates solely to the members or to former members of the body or to persons who have regular contact with it in connection with its purposes and that the personal data are not disclosed outside that body without the consent of the data subjects;"*

Necessary in the interests of public health on the basis of law

Until 2020, the application of this lawful basis was less frequent. It would apply to reportable health and safety incidents and to outbreaks of reportable illnesses as required by law, which became a more common occurrence with the Covid-19 pandemic and the introduction of new laws designed to protect the public from infection.

Necessary for legal obligations/rights

While Article 6 includes a lawful basis that allows the processing of personal data where it is necessary for compliance with a legal obligation to which the controller is subject, this Article 9 lawful basis is slightly different; it only applies to laws that come under the headings of employment law, or social security law, or social protection law.

In addition though, it also applies to processing necessary for the exercising of anyone's rights under these laws, as well as the obligations of the controller.

Explicit consent

Again, the lawful bases in Article 9 are presented with consent first, but it should still be the last resort, and only relied on when none of the other bases are appropriate, and it is unlikely that consent can be classed as freely-given when it is requested by a data subject's landlord or employer.

The standard for consent in Article 9 is higher than in Article 6: it must be *explicit consent,* which in practice means an action must be undertaken to confirm the consent is valid, as well as the consent request being clear and unambiguous, and the consent itself being freely-given.

Consent can be spoken, or a box can be ticked by the data subject, but it should be very clear to the data subject what they are consenting to, and if spoken, a record of the consent – and how and when it was provided – should be kept, for an audit trail.

Substantial Public Interest

The DPA 2018, schedule 1, part 2 lists the circumstances that are considered as being in the 'substantial public interest' from (UK)GDPR Article 9, but the word 'necessary' still features and is a high bar.

It is crucial to read the detail of each paragraph under the headings of the Substantial Public Interest lawful bases, as the heading doesn't always tell the full story.

For example paragraph 18, Safeguarding of children and of individuals at risk, only applies in very specific circumstances, although the term 'safeguarding' can be applied to a wide set of activities.

Not all activities classed as safeguarding would fall under the lawful basis, as it only applies when:

> *"the data processing is necessary for the purposes of—*
>
> *(i) protecting an individual from neglect or physical, mental or emotional harm, or*
>
> *(ii) protecting the physical, mental or emotional well-being of an individual,*
>
> *the individual is—*
>
> *(i) aged under 18, or*
>
> *(ii) aged 18 or over and at risk,*
>
> *...[and] the processing is carried out without the consent of the data subject for one of the reasons listed...*
>
> *(a) in the circumstances, consent to the processing cannot be given by the data subject;*
>
> *(b) in the circumstances, the controller cannot reasonably be expected to obtain the consent of the data subject to the processing;*
>
> *(c) the processing must be carried out without the consent of the data subject because obtaining the consent of the data subject would prejudice the provision of the protection"*

[DPA2018, Schedule 1, Part 2, Paragraph 18]

Therefore, to rely on this lawful basis, the data processing must be designed to protect a particular individual and the person whose data is being processed cannot be expected to provide consent – if they are the child or vulnerable person themselves – or they can't be asked for consent without it prejudicing the safeguarding itself – if they are suspected of causing the child or vulnerable person some harm, or potential harm.

There are many other lawful purposes for processing under substantial public interest in the DPA2018, and below are some of the most relevant for social housing providers.

"Doping in sport" for example, isn't likely to come up in housing, but it is listed in the DPA2018 Schedule 1, Part 2. Some examples that are used with some frequency in social housing include:

6. Statutory etc and government purposes

8. Equality of opportunity or treatment (see chapter 13 for more on EDI data.)

9. Racial and ethnic diversity at senior levels of organisations (see chapter 13 for more on EDI data.)

10. Preventing or detecting unlawful acts

11. Protecting the public against dishonesty etc

12. Regulatory requirements relating to unlawful acts and dishonesty etc

13. Journalism etc in connection with unlawful acts and dishonesty etc

14. Preventing fraud

15. Suspicion of terrorist financing or money laundering

16. Support for individuals with a particular disability or medical condition

17. Counselling etc

18. Safeguarding of children and of individuals at risk

19. Safeguarding of economic well-being of certain individuals

20. Insurance

21. Occupational pensions

[DPA2018, Schedule 1]

Requirement for an appropriate policy document

It is important to note that, to rely on any of the purposes listed under substantial public interest in the DPA2018 Schedule 1, Part 2, the organisation is required to have an 'appropriate policy document' in place first. The policy document is required to explain the procedures in place that (should!) ensure all the (UK)GDPR principles (Article 5) are complied with when personal data is processed based on the lawful bases listed under 'substantial public interest', and indicate how long that data will be retained.

The only relevant exceptions to this requirement are for *'Preventing or detecting unlawful acts'* and for *'Journalism etc in connection with unlawful acts and dishonesty etc'*, when data can lawfully be disclosed – to the authorities or to journalists, as appropriate – for these purposes, without an appropriate policy document being in place first.

In addition, if relying on the Article 9 lawful basis of *"necessary for legal obligations and rights under employment law, social protection law, or social security law"*, the DPA2018 Schedule 1 includes an extra requirement to have an 'appropriate policy document in place' covering that data processing too.

In practice, the 'appropriate policy document' does not need to be one standalone document that covers all data processing that requires such a policy; it may already exist across various policies in the organisation, or it may make sense to create a few new policies instead of just one.

Lawful basis for processing Criminal Information

Article 10 of the (UK)GDPR states that this data can only be lawfully processed either "*in an official capacity*", meaning by official authorities including the police and those with powers of investigation and prosecution, or "*when the processing is authorised by... law providing for appropriate safeguards...*"

This means, for registered providers with no official capacity to prosecute, the purpose for processing criminal information must meet either a condition in Schedule 1, Part 2 of the DPA2018 – the substantial public interest conditions – or one of the *additional* conditions listed in Schedule 1, Part 3 of the DPA2018.

Interestingly, Part 3 also tells us that the Part 2 conditions can be applied even if the processing is not actually judged to be "*in the substantial public interest.*" And for clarity, Part 3 states that, despite Part 2 paragraph 20 Insurance only allowing certain types of personal data to be processed for the specific purposes it describes, that is extended to include criminal information if it is necessary to process criminal information for the insurance purposes as outlined in paragraph 20.

The additional conditions for the lawful processing of criminal information that are most likely to apply to social housing providers' work are:

- The processing is necessary for protecting an individual's vital interests and the data subject is physically or legally incapable of giving consent,

- The processing is of personal data in the public domain, which is manifestly made public by the data subject themselves,

- The processing is necessary for legal claims, legal proceedings (including prospective legal proceedings), obtaining legal advice, or otherwise exercising or defending legal rights,

- Judicial acts, when a court or tribunal is acting in its judicial capacity, and

- Consent is given by the data subject to the processing.

Due to the sensitive nature of criminal information, any existing policies or procedures that involve the processing, or potential processing, of criminal information should be carefully reviewed to ensure a robust lawful basis has been identified and documented.

CHAPTER SIX

DATA SUBJECTS' RIGHTS

All data subjects – customers, employees, stakeholders, the public, or anyone else – have the following legal rights, under the (UK)GDPR:

- The right to be informed about how and why their data is being processed.
- The right of access to copies of their data and some additional information, with some exceptions (DSARs – see below.)
- The right to rectification of errors in their personal data.
- The right to erasure of their personal data, in some circumstances.
- The right to restrict the processing of their personal data, in some circumstances.
- The right to data portability, in some circumstances.
- The right to object to the processing of their personal data.
- The right to not be subject to automated decisions or profiling which has a legal effect (or other significant effect.)

Breaching individuals' rights have the same risks as breaching any other part of the GDPR.

Monetary penalties would theoretically be one potential outcome, but in recent times, fines aren't the highest risk or cost of non-compliance, especially in social housing – it's harm to people, plus the time and other resources involved in handling queries, complaints, increased numbers of data subject requests, and compensation claims.

Receiving rights requests

Any employee could receive a rights request, including a DSAR, in any format – including spoken or over social media – and should ensure the request is handled without delay. In many landlords, the Data Protection Officer (DPO) or their team will coordinate responses to all requests to exercise rights, but they will need colleagues in various teams to cooperate and support them.

In theory, if the (UK)GDPR Principles are followed there should be less need for data subjects to exercise some of their rights.

Complying with the principles also makes some of the rights requests easier to deal with. In particular, complying with the principle of 'data retention' and not retaining excess data, makes data subject access requests (DSARs) easier to respond to as there is less data to review, redact and provide copies of. See below for more information on DSARs.

The rights are not all blanket rights, and there are exceptions in many circumstances.

The law requires that requests are responded to as soon as possible, and within one month at the latest, unless an extension can be applied. See the DSARs section below for information on extensions.

In most cases, rights requests must be responded to free of charge. See the DSARs section below for information on charging for, or refusing, a request.

The right to rectification (Art. 16)

If the principle of 'data accuracy' is complied with, meaning that data is accurate and up to date, data subjects shouldn't need to exercise their right to rectification, for example.

This right is requested on a frequent basis, as part of general customer service, which is to be expected; landlords want to hold accurate and up to date data about their customers.

However, controls must be put in place to ensure only the data subject themselves, or an authorised third-party, can request and make changes to a resident's details.

The right to erasure (Art. 17)

This right, also known as the right to be forgotten, doesn't apply to any data the controller still has a valid and lawful reason for retaining. The right exists to enable data subjects to require the organisation to apply the retention principle to their data in particular (if the data has been retained too long.)

Many controllers will be holding onto personal data longer than their retention schedules state, but a request for erasure from a data subject will only apply to deleting that individual data subject's own data, where there is no longer a valid reason to keep it.

A request like that might raise awareness that data retention schedules have not been followed, and ideally the controller would then implement data deletion or destruction of all the old data, but a request for erasure from a single data subject doesn't require it.

The right to restrict processing (Art. 18)

This right is often exercised for practical reasons, linked to one or more of the other rights. The use of the personal data in question should be restricted – meaning nothing is done to it or with it unless it with the data subject's consent, or is necessary for "*the establishment, exercise or defence of legal claims or for the protection of the rights of another natural or legal person or for reasons of important public interest.*" *[Art. 18 (UK)GDPR]*

The processing must be restricted – at least temporarily – in the following circumstances:

- The data subject claims the personal data is inaccurate, to allow the organisation to verify the accuracy, or otherwise.
- The data is being processed unlawfully, but the data subject chooses restriction over erasure of the data.
- The organisation no longer needs the personal data for its own processing purposes, but the data subject has requested the data is held onto for their purposes of establishing, exercising or defending legal claims.
- The data subject has objected to the processing of the personal data that's been based on legitimate interests, and the organisation needs to verify, or otherwise, whether its own legitimate interests override the interests of the data subject.

The right to data portability (Art. 20)

This right only applies in limited circumstances. If the personal data has been supplied to the organisation directly from the data subject in question, the lawful basis for the processing is 'consent' or 'contract', and the processing is carried out *"by automated means"* (i.e. not paper-only records) the data should be provided to the data subject, upon request, in a *"structured, commonly used and machine-readable format"* (a spreadsheet would fulfil the requirements). The data subject can send the data onto another controller themselves or request that the organisation sends it directly to the other controller, if it's technically able to.

In housing, this right could be requested by a resident wanting their tenancy information such as payments history, for example, for their own analysis or for moving to a new landlord.

The right to object (Art. 21)

The right of a data subject to object to the processing of their personal data is not a blanket right, and the individual's circumstances and reasons for objecting must be considered, unless it relates to direct marketing. If the objection is to processing for "direct marketing purposes", the objection automatically stands and the marketing related processing must stop.

If the processing is based on the lawful basis of either 'public interest task or official function' or 'legitimate interests', and the purpose of the processing is anything other than direct marketing, the data subject can object to the processing on grounds relating to their own personal situation. In that case, the controller must stop processing the data unless it can demonstrate compelling grounds (which are fair, lawful and transparent of course) that override the data subject's interests, rights and freedoms.

An exception to this right, is when data processing is necessary for a task carried out in the public interest, and the data is processed for the purposes of scientific or historical research, or statistical purposes, as laid down in Article 89(1) of the (UK)GDPR. In that case, the processing may continue despite the objection.

In the social housing sector, controllers may prefer to agree to requests to object to processing (and then erase the data) even if the (UK)GDPR does not require it, for customer and employee relations.

It seems a little ironic, that in weighing up the requirement to stop processing, the controller will likely need to collect more personal information about the data subject, to understand their particular reason for objecting. So any objection to processing should be handled sensitively.

Data Subject Access Requests (DSARs) (Art. 15)

The rights request received by most controllers in the housing sector is a Data Subject Access Request (DSAR). Data subjects have the right to receive:

- Confirmation that their data is being processed by the organisation,
- Access to that personal data, and
- Supplementary Information about the processing of that data.

A DSAR must be responded to without delay and in most cases within one month from receiving a valid request, although the timescale can be extended. In most cases it must also be responded to free of charge.

Deliberately withholding or destroying data from a SAR that *should* be released is an offence and the individual responsible – not the controller – could be prosecuted and fined.

In some cases it may feel like the ideal first step after receiving a DSAR would be to hop into a time machine, go back in time, and stop anyone writing any notes or emails they're not happy to share with the data subject who's made the DSAR. Or perhaps even change the way the data subject was treated so they have no reason to be suspicious of the organisation, and no reason to make a DSAR looking for evidence of a conspiracy or similar. Because that is where the motivation for a DSAR often comes from, unfortunately.

In the absence of a time machine, landlords can only put in place good records management practices which will benefit future DSARs, and put in place robust processes for handling DSARs in the here and now.

Receiving a DSAR

A valid DSAR is in any format, not necessarily in writing. This includes spoken requests, requests made face-to-face, by email, text message or over social media or telephone, as well as letter. A DSAR could be received by any member of staff in the first instance, and it should be treated as urgent and logged as a DSAR without delay.

Some organisations choose to provide a form that DSAR applicants can fill in, but under the law, requestors cannot be obliged to fill in a form. In practice, being asked to take extra steps can result in a request for more data than the original DSAR, as it can make requestors understandably annoyed, and even suspicious.

To be valid, a DSAR does *not* need to refer to data protection legislation or be described as a data subject access request. If it is asking for access to personal information for, or on behalf of, the data subject themselves, it must be treated by the organisation as a DSAR.

A DSAR is usually made by the data subject themselves, but they can authorise someone else to make the SAR on their behalf.

Timescale

Holidays and weekends must be included within the one-month deadline for responding to a DSAR, and cannot be used to extend the timescale.

For example, if a DSAR is received on 23 December, the response must be provided by 23 January at the latest, despite the Christmas holidays.

For complex or multiple requests the organisation can extend the timescale by up to another two months, but this would only be in limited circumstances and the landlord should explain to the data subject as soon as possible (and always within one month of the request) why the extension is necessary. The law does not require the controller to seek permission to apply an extension; the reasons should be *explained*, but the data subject cannot object or withhold permission as permission is not required.

Verify identity or authority

If a DSAR comes directly from the data subject, their identity should be verified in the most appropriate way. Based on the relationship with the data subject, the housing provider should adapt their verification processes as appropriate. For example, if the requestor is a current tenant or employee, verification checks could be less stringent, using the current records to check details against. For former tenants and employees, or anyone else, or if there is *any doubt* about the validity of a request, the verification checks should be more stringent, for example requesting a copy of photo ID such as a passport or driving licence, *plus* proof of address such as a recent utility bill.

If the request is being made on behalf of someone else, proof of authority should be provided, which is usually a signed letter or form, unless there is good reason such as disability or incapacity for the request to be verified in another way, e.g. a Lasting Power of Attorney (LPA).

Checking ID should not be used as a tactic to delay a DSAR, but it is *crucial* to be confident that a request is valid before providing any information. It is less risky to delay the fulfilment of a DSAR while double checking the identity or authorisation of a requestor, than to potentially provide information to someone who is pretending to be the data subject, or pretending to have the data subject's authorisation.

Excessive or unfounded DSARs

Requests that are manifestly unfounded or excessive can legally be charged for or refused. The housing provider should include in their DSAR policy which is the preferred response; it is often refusal, as the amount that can be charged is unlikely to cover the actual costs.

This will only apply in very limited circumstances and, if in any doubt, advice should be sought when assessing whether requests may be considered unfounded or excessive.

The criteria to consider when assessing a request as manifestly unfounded or excessive include the data subject's apparent intent, for example if the DSAR is being used as a bargaining chip or way to harass individuals, and the nature of the data requested, for example if it is likely to assist the data subject or if it is repetitive and does not contain much information. It is important to note, however, that the ICO guidance highlights that a DSAR cannot be automatically considered excessive just because the response would include a large amount of data.

Responding to a DSAR

When a request has been identified as valid – it's clearly a DSAR and identity has been verified as appropriate – the one-month clock is ticking and it must be logged and responded to without delay.

The controller, often the DPO (or a colleague of the DPO) acting on behalf of the controller, should log the request, and send an acknowledgement to the DSAR requestor. Acknowledgement letters should *not* assure the requestor that all or any of the data they have requested will be provided, only that they will receive a response to their DSAR within one month and that the organisation will let them know if a time extension will be applied. The acknowledgement letter could also explain that exemptions may well be applied to the information in question and, if appropriate, that some of the information requested isn't within the scope of a DSAR, to manage expectations.

It can be useful to have a template letter available for acknowledgement letters.

The colleague responsible for coordinating the response should begin to gather the information required from relevant business areas, usually by contacting all relevant teams to ask for the information.

The organisation does not necessarily need to provide exactly what has been asked for, if the requested data is out of scope for a DSAR or the data requested would be exempt from the DSAR.

When searching for data to be reviewed and possibly included in the DSAR response, the controller is *not* obliged to carry out searches the way the requestor may have instructed, and it's not always ideal to start off the process with a huge e-discovery which often brings up an overwhelming amount of documents to sift through.

It is often more reasonable to start with a manual search of the files where the data subject's personal data is most likely to be found.

All formats of personal data are in scope; hard copy and electronic, emails, documents, photographs and CCTV/video footage.

Data to be withheld in full

The legal right of access covers only the data subject's own personal data, meaning data from which they can be identified *and* that relates to them. The data subject could still be identifiable in the case of a conversation between two people about the data subject, when the participants know they are talking about that particular individual.

A name is not always required to make data "personal" and conversely, the inclusion of a name does not always mean the data is "personal".

Anything that is *not* the data subject's own personal data can usually be withheld, including business information, policies and procedures, generic emails which the data subject received or was copied into but do not relate directly to them, and data which is solely another person's personal data (known as third party data). For data relating to both the data subject and a third party, see the redaction section below.

Even if the data subject is identifiable, and even if their name is included in a document, if the content of the document is not actually about the data subject, it is not usually their data.

For example, an email that goes to a whole team reminding them of upcoming team meeting dates, or to the whole organisation asking for people to buy raffle tickets. If the only data that is linked to the data subject in the document is their name, in those examples and similar, it would not need to be included in the DSAR response.

There is one exception to this: If the organisation has copies of emails that do not relate to the data subject, but they were processed for a secondary purpose, they could contain the data subject's personal data. For example, if a 'business-as-usual' email was saved especially to review the data subject's work performance, the email would likely be classed as the data subject's personal data, at least to some extent.

Duplicated *data* – not just duplicate documents – can be withheld, and redaction can be done in *any* way appropriate, including extracting the data which is being shared and putting it into a new document. The right of access is to *data, not documents.*

For example, the organisation may have handwritten notes and the typed-up version; as long as they are providing the same information in essence, only one of the versions needs to provided.

Data to be redacted

Several exemptions apply to the right of access, but care must be taken when applying them, and advice sought as necessary.

The right to access is to know what data the organisation has said about the data subject, not which individuals have said those things. So, in general, third-party data can be withheld/redacted unless you have valid consent from the third-party to disclose it (see chapter x about consent), or it is reasonable in the circumstances to disclose it in response to the SAR, even without consent.

If it is reasonable, in the circumstances, to disclose the third party's data to the data subject, it does not need to be redacted. It might be reasonable to keep other people's data in if it is data the data subject has already seen, and would not cause any unreasonable harm or discomfort to the third-party if it is disclosed to the data subject.

Other data which may be redacted or withheld includes information that relates to *"Management forecasting or planning"*, that would be likely to prejudice the organisation's ability to carry out its work.

Other data which may be redacted or withheld includes anything that relates to the organisation's intentions regarding any ongoing negotiations with the data subject, to the extent that disclosing that data would likely prejudice the ongoing negotiations. Please note, this has narrower criteria than the Management Planning one above.

Other exemptions are listed in Schedule 2 of the DPA2018, Parts 2, 3 and 4 and should be carefully reviewed before applying them.

A good rule of thumb though, is:

If in doubt, leave it out!

Information can always be provided later, if it should have been provided, but it can't easily be recovered if it was sent in error.

Sending the data to the data subject

If the request is made electronically, the information must be provided in an electronic format, but it if appropriate the controller can ask the data subject first if they would prefer electronic or hard copy if it is easier to provide the data in hard copy.

Once the relevant data has been collated and redacted and is ready to be disclosed, it must be sent *securely*. To explain the DSAR response to the data subject, it should be accompanied by a letter that explains the data subject is receiving the data they are legally entitled to, so there may be some information they were expecting to see that is not included, due to the application of legal exemptions. The exemptions should be explained in as much detail as possible without giving away too much about exactly what has been redacted.

The letter is required to also include the *"supplementary information"*, which may (and should!) also be found in the organisation's Privacy Notice:

(Bonus tip – this is an ideal chance to check the contents of the Privacy Notice!)

- the purposes of the processing of the data subject's personal data;
- the categories of personal data concerned;
- the recipients (or categories of recipient) to whom the personal data have been or will be disclosed, in particular recipients in third countries or international organisations (and the appropriate safeguards that are in place if the data is transferred to third countries);
- where possible, the period for which the personal data will be stored, or, if not possible, the criteria used to determine that period;
- the existence of the right to request rectification or erasure of their personal data, or restriction of the processing of their personal data, or to object to such processing;

- the right to lodge a complaint with the Information Commissioner, and how to escalate a complaint with the controller, in the first instance;

- where the personal data was not collected from the data subject, any available information as to the source of the data; and

- the existence of automated decision-making, including profiling, that could have legal or similarly significant effects on the data subject, and meaningful information about the logic involved, as well as the significance and the envisaged consequences of such processing for the data subject.

Rights around profiling and automated decision making (Art. 22)

Automated decision-making means making a decision solely by automated means without any human involvement; and

Profiling means automated processing of personal data to evaluate certain things about an individual.

Profiling can be part of an automated decision-making process.

The (UK)GDPR imposes controls around profiling and automated decisions, in order to protect people from negative impacts and unfair treatment. There are two types of profiling/automated decisions, with different rules for each.

The two types are defined by the impact on data subjects, as a result of the profiling/automated decisions:

- High risk profiling/automated decisions that produce legal or similarly significant effects. This is covered by Article 22 of the (UK)GDPR.

  An example would be using a formula or algorithm to decide

whether or not to offer an applicant a tenancy, based on information about them.

- Other profiling/automated decisions which have less significant effects on data subjects, but there are still rules around how to approach it.

  An example would be targeting individuals for marketing, based on information about them.

All profiling and automated decision-making

As with all data processing, all requirements of the (UK)GDPR must be complied with, including the principles, and upholding the rights of data subjects involved.

If, as is likely, the lawful basis for using profiling and/or automated decisions is either "public interest task or functions" or "legitimate interests", the controller must ensure there is a process that allows data subjects to object to the processing.

If the profiling is linked to sending direct marketing messages, the processing must stop immediately upon receipt of an object, in relation to that data subject.

Best practice when implementing any profiling or automated decision-making includes the use of appropriate mathematical or statistical procedures, putting measures in place to identify and correct any errors and minimise risks, keep the data secure, and prevent discrimination.

High risk profiling and automated decision-making (Art. 22)

High risk profiling or automated decision-making, that has legal or similar significant effects on data subjects, is lawful only on the basis of valid consent from the data subjects concerned, or if it is necessary for a contract with the individual, or if it is authorised by law (and appropriate safeguards are in place.)

High risk profiling should not involve children.

Before doing high risk profiling/automated decision-making, a data protection impact assessment (DPIA) must be carried out. (See chapter 9 on DPIAs.)

The use of special categories of personal data in high-risk profiling/automated decision-making is lawful only on the basis of *explicit* consent from the data subject, or it is necessary for a substantial public interest, on the basis of law (and appropriate safeguards are in place.) An Article 6 lawful basis must be identified as well.

When the organisation is collecting the data that will be profiled/used to make automated decisions, data subjects must be informed of:

- The existence of the profiling/automated decisions,
- The consequences of the processing, and
- Meaningful information about the logic involved.

When responding to a DSAR, if any of the data involved has been processed for the purposes of high-risk profiling/automated decisions, the requestor must be informed of:

- The existence of the high-risk profiling/automated decisions, and
- The consequences of the processing.

In addition to the usual data subject rights (see chapter 6), when high-risk profiling/automated decisions are in place, the organisation must have a simple process that allows data subjects to:

- Express their opinion about the outcome,
- Obtain human intervention, and
- Challenge a decision.

This does not necessarily mean that the outcome will be changed, but it should be reviewed by a human, who may change the outcome, or confirm it.

CHAPTER SEVEN

INTERNATIONAL DATA TRANSFERS

Because data subjects could lose the protection their data would (or should!) have around their data and how it is processed, if the data is transferred outside of the UK, the legislation contains requirements for what are known as 'restricted transfers' of data, or 'international transfers.'

These requirements, laid down in Chapter V of the (UK)GDPR, aim to ensure that personal data has the same or equivalent level of legal protection when it is transferred outside of the geographical scope of the (UK)GDPR.

A transfer of personal data is a 'restricted transfer' when the data is being sent by one organisation to another organisation, that could be either a controller or processor, which is a legally separate organisation, and is outside of the UK. This includes companies who are in the same group structure but are distinct legal entities.

When a transfer is NOT a restricted transfer

Sending personal data to an employee of a UK-based controller, when that employee is working remotely, outside of the UK but using the organisation's usual systems with its appropriate security measures in place, is not a restricted transfer.

If a controller contracts with a data processor (see chapter x on data processors) that is a UK-based company, and that processor contracts with a sub-processor company which is based outside of the UK, even if the controller transfers their data directly to the non-UK sub-processor, the controller is not carrying out a restricted transfer. In that situation, the processor is carrying out a restricted transfer, because they have entered into the contract with the non-UK sub-processor. The processor is responsible for controlling the restricted transfer lawfully and securely.

When data is simply routed through a non-UK country on its way from one UK organisation to another UK organisation, that is not regarded as a restricted transfer, or a transfer at all.

When a transfer is a restricted transfer

In the UK housing sector, restricted transfers will most often occur when contracting with data processors located outside of the UK. Many software providers are based outside of the UK, often based in the USA.

When considering what controls are required around a restricted transfer, controllers should first of all consider if there is another option, such as a UK-based company, or an EAA-based company.

The EEA countries are currently covered by adequacy decisions, meaning that transfers to those countries are regarded as providing 'adequate protection', equivalent to the UK legal protections, and no further specific controls are needed, other than the usual compliance with the (UK)GDPR requirements.

At the time of writing, the following countries also have findings of adequacy:

Andorra, Argentina, Guernsey, Isle of Man, Israel, Jersey, New Zealand, Switzerland and Uruguay.

In addition, there are partial findings of adequacy about:

- Japan; the adequacy decision only covers private sector organisations.

- Canada; the adequacy decision only covers data that is subject to Canada's Personal Information Protection and Electronic Documents Act (PIPEDA). Not all data is subject to PIPEDA.

If there is no adequacy decision

The controller should assess whether the restricted transfer can be carried out with "appropriate safeguards". The first step is to undertake a Transfer Risk Assessment, assessing the risks to data subjects involved by transferring their personal data to the (non-adequate) country.

For UK social housing providers, carrying out restricted transfers due to something like entering into a contract with software providers in a non-adequate country, the transfer mechanism in Article 46 of the (UK)GDPR that is available to them, following a Transfer Risk Assessment, is using Standard Data Protection Contractual Clauses (not to be confused with Data Processor contract clauses) that both the transferring organisation and the recipient enter into.

Due to Brexit, this mechanism is currently in the process of transitioning from the existing "Standard Contractual Clauses" from the EU legislation, to an "IDTA" (International Data Transfer Agreement) in the UK legislation. The two formats are co-existing for a limited period. The contents of the templates must be applied without any changes.

Transferring organisations can use the UK International Data Transfer Agreement (IDTA) template, or the IDTA Addendum (known as the "Addendum") alongside the new standard contractual clauses (SCCs) that were issued by the European Commission under the EU GDPR on 04 June 2021. The new EU SCCs are not valid for restricted transfers from the UK on their own; the Addendum must be used as well.

For contracts which were entered into prior to 21 September 2022, which contained the old EU SCCs, the old EU SCCs continue to be valid for restricted transfers from the UK, but only until 21 March 2024.

From 21 March 2024, if the restricted transfers are to continue, the transferring organisation and recipient must enter into a new contract that includes either the IDTA or the new SCCs and the Addendum.

It is important to note that, even with an IDTA or the SCCs and Addendum in place, the Transfer Risk Assessment must be carried out to assess whether the personal data being transferred will actually be protected appropriately. If the IDTA or the SCCs plus Addendum will not provide the legally required level of control and protection as they are, the transferring organisation should put in place additional controls before agreeing to transfer, or transferring, any data.

The risk assessment is certainly not straightforward, but the ICO currently has guidance on its website.

CHAPTER EIGHT

DATA SHARING AND DATA PROCESSORS & CONTROLLERS

Data Sharing

Personal data sharing is a form of processing and so personal data must only be shared with third parties when the sharing has one or more appropriate lawful bases, and is carried out in keeping with the data protection principles and while upholding the rights of data subjects.

This includes sharing with other data controllers such as other agencies and organisations that social housing providers often work with, such as local authorities, the police, and charities.

There are many lawful bases that will allow a housing provider to share data with another organisation, without the consent of the data subject, but that does not mean the landlord is obliged to provide the information; especially where the lawful basis is "legitimate interests" it is crucial to weigh up the potential impact on the data subject compared to the interests of the organisation or the recipient organisation.

For example, a utilities supplier may request a forwarding address for a former resident, and while it may be possible to validate that as being necessary for the legitimate interests of the utilities company, the landlord may not have enough information about the individual's specific circumstances to be able to assess the potential impact on the from sharing that forwarding address, meaning a comprehensive legitimate interests assessment cannot be carried out, in order to rely on legitimate interests as the lawful basis.

It is useful for landlords to decide on standard policies and have guidance in place for colleagues to refer to when they receive routine requests for data, or want to request data from another organisation.

They should lay out the purposes and types of data, and data subjects, that it is likely to be appropriate to share data with other agencies about, in particular circumstances, on a lawful basis. The other principles will all need to be complied with as well, of course, which is easy to disregard if faced with a request from someone in authority. For example, it is important to be comfortable with the amount of data being requested, even if it is a request from the police or the NHS, as it is not unknown for agencies to request excessive amounts of data.

Coming back to the utilities company, it is appropriate and lawful for landlords to make it their standard policy to not provide forwarding addresses to utility suppliers.

In contrast though, it is just as important that colleagues understand that data protection law does not prevent the organisation from sharing personal data if there is a valid purpose such as protecting a vulnerable individual, and the sharing is necessary in the circumstances.

Data can be shared lawfully between organisations without a Data Sharing Agreement in place, as long as the (UK)GDPR requirements are complied with. Some organisations though, will insist on an Agreement being in place before they will share data.

Data Sharing Agreements

A landlord may enter into Data Sharing Agreements (DSAs) with other data controllers, but the sharing still needs one or more appropriate lawful basis, because signing up to a DSA does *not* in and of itself make sharing legal. A DSA is usually put in place between organisations that are controllers in their own rights, and is designed to explain what circumstances are likely to be lawful for data sharing, and might include agreed practical issues such as how many lines of address will be shared, or what emails would be used to share the data between the organisations.

Data Controllers and Processors

The housing provider is usually the Controller – a Controller is the legal entity that determines the purposes and means of processing the personal data in question.

Landlords can't do everything in the business themselves, so buy in help from suppliers.

If a supplier will, or could, touch the personal data the Landlord controls, as part of the service they provide and sell, and the supplier can only do what the controller tells them to do with that data, that supplier is a data processor working on behalf of the controller.

Examples include:

- Web developers & hosts
- CRM providers
- Bulk Email system providers
- HR consultants and providers
- Outsourced payroll providers
- CCTV operators
- Archiving and shredding providers
- IT consultants
- Data Protection consultants

In some circumstances, a housing provider may be a processor for another controller. For example, providing a housing management service for other property owners, depending on the nature of the agreement.

Suppliers who are controllers in their own right

A minority of suppliers who will, or could, touch the controller's personal data as part of the service they provide will be able to decide what to do with that data – or at least some of it – themselves, because they are a controller in their own right.

A prime example is recruitment specialists. They are finding candidates for several organisations, and to have on their own books, not just sending the candidates to an individual housing provider. They are the controllers of the candidates' data.

There are no legal requirements to include in a contract between individual Controllers (unless the parties are Joint Controllers – see below), but it is good practice to at least identify the parties to the contract as controllers in their own right and highlight the key legal data protection obligations they each have.

Processor or Controller?

Identifying whether a supplier is a processor or controller in its own right is based on which organisation instigates the collection of the data and decides how and why it is used.

It is the same with processors and controllers; if the supplier would collect – and be in control of – the same specific data for their own purposes anyway, whether it was being paid by the landlord for the service or not, it is a controller in its own right.

Data Processor Contracts

Article 28 of the (UK)GDPR lays out the clauses that should be included in a Data Processor (DP) contract. But the legal requirements actually start one step earlier.

Article 28 of the (UK)GDPR also states that:

"the controller shall use only processors providing sufficient guarantees to implement appropriate technical and organisational measures in such a manner that processing will meet the requirements of this Regulation and ensure the protection of the rights of the data subject." [Art. 28, (UK)GDPR]

Therefore, carrying out appropriate due diligence on the data protection and data security capabilities on any potential supplier is a crucial first step.

Once a supplier has been selected, the appropriate data processing clauses will protect the client from liability if the processor is responsible for a data security breach or any other breach of the (UK)GDPR.

In essence, the Article 28 clauses require that a processor will:

- only act on the controller's instructions, unless legally required to do something else;
- ensure the people doing the processing are subject to a duty of confidence;
- take appropriate security measures;
- engage sub-processors only with the controller's authorisation and on the basis of a written contract with the same processor clauses;
- allow for audits of the data processing;

- assist the controller in responding to requests from Data Subjects, or data breaches, and in carrying out Data Protection Impact Assessments; and

- return or delete all Personal Data at the end of the contract, as required by the client/controller.

Sub-processors

Controllers must give (or not) their authorisation to the processor for the use of sub-processors, but this doesn't have to be on a case-by-case basis. The processor contract could state, for example, that "the Processor is authorised to appoint sub-processors as necessary, on the basis that the sub-processor provides sufficient guarantees to implement appropriate technical and organisational measures in such a manner that processing will meet legal requirements, and on the basis of a written contract containing clauses relating to processing that are manifestly equivalent to the clauses in this contract."

Processing Instructions or Schedule of Processing

As well as the standard clauses from Article 28, the contract must include specific instructions about the type of data processing to be carried out by the supplier/processor. These details are often included in what is known as a Schedule of Processing.

Ideally, this would be bespoke to every contract, but in practical terms, general sets of instructions can be used for various types of contract. A housing provider may have a template schedule of processing for software providers, one for building contractors, and one for consultants, for example.

Obligations of the Controller

The contract must also identify the obligations of the controller. How much detail this should involve isn't specified, but the contract will often state, for example:

"The Controller will comply with its obligations under data protection law, including being responsible for responding to Data Subject requests and reporting reportable data breaches."

Lawful basis

As with any processing of personal data, the controller must comply with all the principles of the (UK)GDPR, in Article 5.

The first principle requires all personal data processing to be fair, lawful and transparent. Processing is only lawful if it meets one of the lawful bases from Article 6. However, when appointing a processor, the processor 'inherits' the lawful basis from the controller, so there is no need to identify a separate lawful basis for sharing the data with your Processor.

The other requirements of the principles must be considered though, before sharing any data with a processor: transparency; purpose limitation; data minimisation; accuracy; storage limitation; security; and accountability.

International Data Transfers

Another key requirement of the (UK)GDPR is that personal data shall not be transferred outside of the UK without one or more of the legal conditions (from Chapter V (UK)GDPR) being met. (See chapter 7 on international data transfers.)

Using processors often results in data being transferred outside of the UK, to servers physically based outside of the UK, and/or to an 'international organisation.'

Red flags in data processor contracts

The key red flag is when data processing clauses have not been included at all, but should have been!

There is no set way that the data processing clauses must be worded or laid out, but controllers should be wary of wording that dilutes the purpose of the clauses; to give the controller control over the processing.

For example, processors may prefer to put long timescales in against the requirement to report data breaches to the client/controller, or make it awkward for the client to audit their data processing.

Other problems that often get missed when contracts with data processor suppliers are reviewed, are conflicting clauses in other sections of the contract. If only the section of the contract headed "Data Protection" is reviewed, there's a real risk of missing conflicting clauses, especially limitation of liabilities and warranties.

Managing processor risks

The size of a supplier/processor doesn't affect the risk, and large companies – that one might expect to know better – often omit appropriate data processing clauses from their standard Terms and Conditions or contracts.

The risk and responsibility for the data processing clauses being in the contract lies with the client/controller; the supplier/processor is *not* breaching the law by excluding data processing clauses, but the client/controller *is.* The client/controller is also potentially breaching the (UK)GDPR by allowing the supplier to access the personal data without a lawful basis.

However, if a supplier processes data for a controller without appropriate data processing clauses in place in the contract, they could be guilty of processing data without a lawful basis (as the lawful basis for processing is 'inherited' by the supplier from the client.)

Buying in services for marketing purposes is particularly high risk for PECR (Privacy and Electronic Communications Regulations) breaches and fines; if a marketer sends messages at the instigation of the client, that require consent, but there is no consent, both the marketer and the client are on the hook for the PECR breach. This includes web developers who don't apply compliant cookie banners. (See chapter 14 on contacting people.)

In practice, if the marketer is based outside of the UK, it may be much easier for the ICO to go after the UK-based client than the marketer.

The suppliers with access to the highest amounts of data, or to particularly sensitive data, are the highest risk, regardless of size of company. So, CRM and HR systems providers, and any cloud storage providers.

Complying with the legal requirements should be non-negotiable and a cost of doing compliant business for the processor, but anything over and above the legal requirements that a controller may wish to include in a supplier contract is a business matter between the two parties.

Be Prepared

Ideally, appropriate contracts should already be in place with anyone that the controller might need in a rush, such as IT crisis support companies. In the case of a cyber-attack housing providers will very likely need a specialist IT firm to go into the systems and servers to do damage control and investigations. Controllers mustn't let anyone, even the best IT companies, do that unless the right contract clauses are in place first, otherwise matters could just get worse!

Joint Controllers

Article 26 of the (UK)GDPR covers the concept of "Joint Controllers", which comes into play when *"two or more controllers jointly determine the purposes and means of processing".*

In the social housing sector, joint controllership arrangements are not common, but may be appropriate in some partnership working arrangements, for example when two or more organisations launch a project together, that is a new service or product for both parties.

When entering into a joint controller arrangement, the (UK)GDPR requires the organisations involved to agree between them their respective responsibilities for complying with the GDPR with regards to any data processing undertaken as part of the arrangement. Article 26 states that the parties shall determine their respective responsibilities *"in particular as regards the exercising of the rights of the data subject and their respective duties to provide"* Privacy Notice information to data subjects, and the controllers can choose to designate a contact point for data subjects. Regardless of what arrangement is made about data subject rights, though, under the (UK)GDPR data subjects can exercise their data subject rights against each of the joint controllers.

The joint controllers are required to make *"the essence of the arrangement"* available to the data subjects in question.

CHAPTER NINE

DATA PROTECTION IMPACT ASSESSMENTS (DPIAs)

In some circumstances the data controller is required by the (UK)GDPR to undertake, and document, a formal DPIA.

The (UK)GDPR Article 35 states:

> *"Where a type of processing in particular using new technologies, and taking into account the nature, scope, context and purposes of the processing, is likely to result in a high risk to the rights and freedoms of natural persons, the controller shall, prior to the processing, carry out an assessment of the impact of the envisaged processing operations on the protection of personal data."*

Leaving aside until later the difficulty of identifying when processing *"is likely to result in a high risk to the rights and freedoms of natural persons"* without carrying out an impact assessment, let's look at what a DPIA should cover.

There is no set format or template for a DPIA, but coming back to the (UK)GDPR:

> *"The assessment shall contain at least:*
>
> *(a) a systematic description of the envisaged processing operations and the purposes of the processing, including, where applicable, the legitimate interest pursued by the controller;*

(b) an assessment of the necessity and proportionality of the processing operations in relation to the purposes;

(c) an assessment of the risks to the rights and freedoms of data subjects referred to in paragraph 1; and

(d) the measures envisaged to address the risks, including safeguards, security measures and mechanisms to ensure the protection of personal data and to demonstrate compliance with this Regulation taking into account the rights and legitimate interests of data subjects and other persons concerned."

[Art. 35 (UK)GDPR]

DPIAs in practice

Before jumping straight into a DPIA though, the ideal first aspect to consider is getting clarity on what the processing is designed to achieve, and just as importantly, whether the processing is even likely to achieve that outcome.

In many circumstances, when the idea of a project or new way of working is considered from the viewpoint of 'purpose', the people planning the project realise that it might not be the best way to achieve the stated purpose, or its purpose might not even align with the organisation's wider purpose and values. A DPIA may not be required then, if the project is abandoned or amended based on the consideration of purpose.

When to carry out a DPIA

Article 35 of the (UK)GDPR also includes specific types of processing which will always require a DPIA to be carried out beforehand. The ones most likely to apply to social housing are processing that involves:

- Large scale processing of special categories of personal data or of criminal information, or

- Large scale monitoring of a publicly accessible area, such as CCTV.

As required by Article 35 of the (UK)GDPR, the ICO has published a list of the types of processing it considers to be likely to result in high risk, which will require a DPIA in most instances. The list is available on the ICO website, and is summarised below.

1. Innovative technology: Data processing that involves the use of innovative technologies, or the innovative application of existing technologies, including AI, when this processing is combined with any of these processes: evaluation or scoring, high-risk automated decision-making, systematic monitoring, sensitive/highly personal data, data processed on a large scale, matching or combining datasets, data about vulnerable data subjects, or preventing data subjects from exercising a right or using a service or contract.

2. Denial of service: Decisions about an individual's access to a product, service, opportunity or benefit that is based to any extent on automated decision-making (including profiling) or involves the processing of special category data.

3. Large-scale profiling: any profiling of individuals on a large scale.

4. Biometrics: any processing of biometric data when this processing is combined with any of these processes: evaluation or scoring, high-risk automated decision-making, systematic monitoring, sensitive/highly personal data, data processed on a large scale, matching or combining datasets, data about vulnerable data subjects, or preventing data subjects from exercising a right or using a service or contract.

5. Genetic data: any processing of genetic data, other than that processed by an individual GP or health professional for the provision of health care direct to the data subject, when this processing is combined with any of these processes: evaluation or scoring, high-risk automated decision-making, systematic

monitoring, sensitive/highly personal data, data processed on a large scale, matching or combining datasets, data about vulnerable data subjects, or preventing data subjects from exercising a right or using a service or contract.

6. Data matching: combining, comparing or matching personal data obtained from multiple sources.

7. Invisible processing: processing of personal data that has not been obtained directly from the data subject and the controller considers that provision of transparent Privacy Notices to the data subjects would be impossible or would involve disproportionate effort, when this processing is combined with any of these processes: evaluation or scoring, high-risk automated decision-making, systematic monitoring, sensitive/highly personal data, data processed on a large scale, matching or combining datasets, data about vulnerable data subjects, or preventing data subjects from exercising a right or using a service or contract.

8. Tracking: processing which involves tracking data subjects' location or behaviour, including online location and behaviour, when this processing is combined with any of these processes: evaluation or scoring, high-risk automated decision-making, systematic monitoring, sensitive/highly personal data, data processed on a large scale, matching or combining datasets, data about vulnerable data subjects, or preventing data subjects from exercising a right or using a service or contract.

9. Targeting of children or other vulnerable individuals: processing the personal data of children or other vulnerable people for marketing purposes, profiling or other automated decision-making.

10. Risk of physical harm: where a personal data breach could risk the physical health or safety of any people.

Then we consider all the ways the processing could impact on the data subjects; including both positive and negative effects, and including if things go to plan, or if the data is breached somehow.

These actions cover points a, b and c above, which brings us to (d) *"the measures envisaged to address the risks..."* This is where we think about what needs to be done in order to protect the personal data of course, but also *"to demonstrate compliance with this Regulation."*

We should be ensuring, for starters, that we're complying with the rest of Article 5(1): data processing that is fair, lawful and transparent; processing is for limited purposes; data minimisation; data accuracy; and storage limitation.

Then there's upholding the rights of data subjects, working with processors if relevant, and dealing effectively with any breaches.

And we should be able to show we've considered all these things, and taken steps to achieve them.

It is safe to say a DPIA is not a simple task; a DPIA is a process to help identify, and manage, the potential impacts of data processing and to help ensure the processing complies with data protection law.

It's helpful to use a template as a starting point for a DPIA, that includes sections for all the questions we've discussed, but be sure to add a little imagination too. It's important to keep an open mind about the processing and especially:

1) the purpose and necessity of the processing, which should be weighed against;

2) the potential negative effects on data subjects.

All decisions relating to the handling of personal data should be assessed for risks, though, even if it doesn't at first appear to obviously fall under the criteria for activities that require a formal DPIA.

The legislation requires that a DPIA is carried out wherever the proposed activity represents a risk to people, so decision-makers need a way to make that initial assessment, before even considering a full DPIA.

A first-phase assessment

As highlighted above, certain types of processing require a DPIA to be undertaken, but it might not be immediately obvious that a project or new way of working will involve data processing of a type that comes under the definitions above, of requiring a DPIA.

Therefore, to ensure all potentially risky data processing is assessed, *all* data-related projects, policies, and procedures should go through at least a first-phase assessment.

In simple terms, a 'data-related' project, policy or procedure is *anything and everything* to do with collecting, using, analysing, sharing, storing or even deleting information that identifies, or can *potentially* identify people.

Which sounds straightforward, but it's not always that simple.

Most people will realise that information containing names is classed as personal data, but will not always realise that asset data or other information that doesn't include a name can also constitute personal data.

(See chapter 3 for more information on the definition of personal data.)

In the social housing sector, some of the projects and policy changes that should be flagged as involving personal data, and therefore needing to be risk assessed from a data protection angle, include:

- Allocation policies and processes
- Equality, diversity and inclusion work and improvement

- Tenant and customer feedback collection
- Complaints management
- Anti-social behaviour (ASB) management
- Rent and arrears collection
- Repairs services
- Evictions
- Stock transfers
- Monitoring of energy use
- Offering advice services such as money advice or help to get into employment.
- Communicating with tenants about such services, or about tenancy matters.
- Employee recruitment
- Performance management
- Managing absences and maternity/paternity/parental/adoption leave
- Administering employee benefits and pensions

The first step to getting housing providers to risk assess all relevant projects and policies is communication; all colleagues who are involved in any of the projects or policies listed above, or anything similar, especially the decision-makers, should be aware of the chances of their project or policy involving personal data, meaning that data protection risks should be considered right from the start.

Ideally, all idea-producing areas of the organisation should be identified. It is vital to consider data protection at the *ideas* stage, *not* the decision-making stages (or even later!).

This could be senior management in general, customer services, ICT or HR teams, a research and development team, a project management team, or a policy team.

Prompts to consider data protection can be added into the paperwork and systems, and onto the agenda of any meetings, where new ideas and plans are discussed.

What should a Data Protection Impact Assessment (DPIA) include?

As explained above, there is no set format or template for a DPIA, but the (UK)GDPR states:

> *"The assessment shall contain at least:*
>
> *(a) a systematic description of the envisaged processing operations and the purposes of the processing, including, where applicable, the legitimate interest pursued by the controller;*
>
> *(b) an assessment of the necessity and proportionality of the processing operations in relation to the purposes;*
>
> *(c) an assessment of the risks to the rights and freedoms of data subjects referred to in paragraph 1; and*
>
> *(d) the measures envisaged to address the risks, including safeguards, security measures and mechanisms to ensure the protection of personal data and to demonstrate compliance with this Regulation taking into account the rights and legitimate interests of data subjects and other persons concerned."*

[Art. 35 (UK)GDPR]

Overlaying these legal requirements with a five-part risk management framework – Recognise, Reduce, Report, Review, Research/Risk assess – (which is also used in chapter 10 on data security and breaches) produces the following steps to work through and use as the basis for the DPIA process:

1. Recognise, including Research and Risk Assessment
    a. Clarify what processing will be undertaken, and its purpose.
    b. Identify the risks to the data subjects, and the organisation.
    c. Assess the proportionality of the processing, given the purpose and the risks.
2. Reduce
    a. Consider controls and measures to reduce the risks.
3. Report
    a. Document the findings, recommendations and agreed actions, feeding into project plan/policy as required.
4. Review
    a. Keep the DPIA under review. A DPIA is a living document, not a static checklist.

How to identify risks

From the above, part 1b, identifying the risks, can be the most challenging part of carrying out a DPIA. Here are some ideas for brainstorming and identifying various risks.

We all have biases and naturally see the world through our own lens. Which can mean we miss the potential impacts of a project or process on people with different life experiences and situations.

To unearth some risks that might not occur immediately, try role playing and imagine how people with different characteristics – gender, age, ethnicity, religion, sexuality, etc. – might be impacted by, or perceive, the processing. Or how someone with ulterior motives could misuse the planned processing.

Another way to identify potential impacts is to think about different life experiences and how that would or could affect a person's view of the processing.

For example, pregnancy is a reason to celebrate for many people, but for others it's linked to fear, anxiety, illness or worse. Some people may be happy to discuss their health, ethnicity, religion, sexuality, etc. but consider the impact that processing these types of data could have on someone who has a hidden disability, or a mental health diagnosis which is often misunderstood, someone who has experienced racial or religious discrimination, or who has reasons for wanting to keep their sexuality private.

Even if the planned processing is designed to have a positive impact, it might not be perceived that way by people who have previously experienced harassment or discrimination because of their personal circumstances. They may have, understandably, lost trust in organisations wanting to collect or process information about their lives.

Take a step back and consider if stereotypes or similar feature in the thinking about the planned processing. We can all easily rely on simple generalisations when thinking about a group of people, such as tenants or customers, people over or under a certain age, men or women, but consider if that is really true of *all* of those people, or is there a risk of upsetting some people by applying such a generalisation?

To recognise potential risks from a process perspective, explore two key areas – where the data goes, and who is involved in touching the data in any way.

Consider if there are any unnecessary data transfers, and what could go wrong. Then think about all the people and organisations involved in the project and/or planned processing.

Are there any conflicts of interest or risk of misuse or breach of data by a disgruntled or stressed employee?

Has due diligence been carried out on any third parties including suppliers, does the contract include data processing clauses, and are there any international transfers and any problematic indemnities, for example?

In many housing providers, the Procurement Policy only requires due diligence and a legal review of the paperwork if the contract is worth more than a certain monetary value. But these checks should be carried out regardless of the value of the contract, if *any* personal data processing will be carried out by a supplier.

Some organisations will already have a risk assessment matrix, but if not, it can be as simple as 3 levels – low, medium, high – or numbers. Consider not only what could go wrong, but what the organisation's risk appetite and tolerance is.

Responsibilities

The Data Protection Officer (DPO) is responsible for giving advice on DPIAs, but the process should be owned and led by the relevant area of the organisation, that is responsible for the project or policy involved.

The DPO may be asked to sign-off a DPIA, but it is not the DPO's responsibility to approve the risks or controls, only to advise and monitor. The DPO may prefer to sign the DPIA to confirm they've given their advice, rather than approval.

How to reduce potential risks

The organisation might be happy to accept some of the risks without implementing all, or any, of the possible controls.

When suggesting controls, this concept can help. A concept called the Hierarchy of Controls is used in Health & Safety. From most to least effective, the list goes:

- Elimination – remove the hazard.
- Substitution – use a less hazardous item, material, liquid, etc.
- Engineering controls – keep people separated from the hazard.
- Administrative controls – policies and procedures.
- PPE – Personal protective equipment.

Granted, face masks and gloves aren't likely to be much use in controlling data-related risks, but the others are certainly worth looking at.

Starting at the top of the list, with the most effective type of control, reflect on whether any data or parts of the processing can be eliminated, or can a less risky process be substituted into the project.

Moving down the hierarchy of controls, an example of an engineering control would be locking data away securely, which can be applied to both physical data storage and electronic data.

Administrative controls include policies and procedures and training. When we think about how many data breaches are linked to human error, when someone hasn't followed the instructions, and has emailed the wrong recipient without double-checking the address for example, it is clear why this is so low down the list of effective controls; procedures and instructions *support* the other controls, not replace them.

If colleagues decide not to follow the DPO's advice on controlling the risks, the organisation's Standing Orders as part of the Governance framework will – hopefully – identify where, and at what level, the acceptance of risks, and overriding of the DPO's advice can be signed off at.

How and when to report on risks, controls & actions

It's important to keep the risks, controls and actions at the forefront of everyone's minds during and after the project as required. Reporting should be to the appropriate internal forums, which will depend on the size of the risk, the likelihood of it materialising, whether it is project-based or ongoing, who owns the risk, and whether it is something the Regulator of Social Housing (or any other regulator) would expect to have reported to them if it materialised.

Reporting of risks should include the controls that have been agreed and put in place, and any other follow-up action, so the effect of the controls and actions can be kept under review.

How to review risks, controls & actions

It's important to continue to monitor the controls, and to understand whether they are controlling the risk effectively, they could/should be improved (and conversely) are they too restrictive.

How often, and for how long, risks and controls are kept under review will be based on whether it is a short-lived risk or an ongoing issue. For stand-alone projects, it is ideal to build the reviews into the project management process. If the risk and controls will exist post-project end, then the maintenance should be built into 'business as usual' review activities.

It's helpful to use a template as a starting point for a DPIA, that includes sections for all the parts above, but be sure to add a little imagination too. It's important to keep an open mind about the processing and especially about the purpose and necessity of the processing, which should be weighed against the potential negative effects on data subjects.

CHAPTER TEN

DATA SECURITY, BREACHES AND COMPLAINTS

Data Security

Many organisations, including housing providers, may be unsure about the risks linked to a potential data breach actually are, especially now the multi-million-pound GDPR fines we were warned about have been few and far between in the UK. It could feel like the pressure is off.

On the other hand, it appears that ransomware attacks are on the rise in all sectors, and a Google of the phrase "housing association data breach" brings up results like "Your data breach could be worth thousands."

Even without the threat of (UK)GDPR fines, a data breach could still cost the organisation many thousands of pounds. Not just paying out on ransoms to cyber-criminals, or compensation to data subjects, but also all the time spent dealing with the incident, and the impact that has on customer relationships and colleague morale.

On top of this, is of course the potential, and very real, harm that could be caused to data subjects whose data is breached, including risk of fraud, scams, harassment, and the worry and stress that goes along with those problems.

Unfortunately there's no easy fix, but there are steps that can reduce and control the risk of it happening, and the impact if (or when!) it happens.

A data security breach can be the result of intentional actions or of inadvertent errors and it can be caused by external or internal factors or people. See chapter 9 on DPIAs for more details on the risks associated with data.

The data security principle uses the word 'appropriate', meaning organisations must decide for themselves what type of security measures to implement.

The legislation does specify that organisations should use both technical and organisational measures to ensure personal data is processed securely, and the (UK)GDPR states that this includes protecting the data from *"unauthorised or unlawful processing, or from accidental loss or damage." [Art. 5 (UK)GDPR]*

Technical measures include systems security, access controls, password policies, use of multi-factor authentication, firewalls, technical resilience, and duplication of systems and servers.

Organisational measures include disaster recovery measures and plans, regular testing of (both technical and organisational) security measures, physical security of premises and data, policies, procedures, training, and audits.

Examples of security measures

Security measures are a huge topic, and can't be covered in full detail here. Here are just a few examples of security measures that should be applied to some degree in the housing sector.

Password Policy: Advice on password policies is always developing, and there are pros and cons for different approaches. At the time of writing, expert advice includes using the 'three random words' technique, and preventing passwords being too short. Experts are advising against caps on password length, and are now advising *against* 'complexity requirements', where passwords are forced to have a mixture of types of character.

Users should be instructed to keep passwords safe, not somewhere they will be easily found, and to never share log-in details and passwords with anyone else.

In addition, organisations are being encouraged to implement multi-factor authentication wherever possible.

Paper: Data protection is often thought of as only applying to electronically held data, so paper records sometime get overlooked when, in fact, losing paper records could more easily lead to an opportunistic data breach as there is no password or multi-factor authentication on a piece of paper.

Paper files containing personal data should be stored in locked filing cabinets or drawers when not in use, and disposed of carefully when no longer used, ideally into a locked receptacle before it is shredded.

Scraps of paper containing names or other personal data should be treated as carefully as if they were a more official document; the risk is in the data it contains, not the format of the paper. Scraps of paper or sticky notes that aren't due to be filed, aren't usually in scope of the data protection legislation (unless the organisation is a public body and is subject to the Freedom of Information Act) but the risk to the people involved is still the same.

Emails: It is so easy to make a mistake when sending emails and cause an accidental data breach. To reduce that risk, reliance on standard email for sharing personal data should be limited where possible.

Many accidental data breaches are caused by hitting 'reply all' on emails, or by sending emails to groups of people in either the 'To' or 'CC' (carbon copy) fields instead of the 'BCC' (blank carbon copy) field.

This can be prevented by using a bulk emailing system, although due diligence and processor contract clauses are essential first (see chapter 8 on using data processors).

However, not every colleague can, nor should they, have access to the organisation's account on a bulk emailing system; a useful alternative is to use the mail merge function, which means drafting an email in a Word document, and sending it to a list of contacts, and every recipient will receive an individual email, with no chance of seeing any other recipient's email address. It is crucial to ensure the contacts list includes only accurate email addresses and names though, of course.

Another common issue is sending an email to the wrong recipient by clicking on the wrong email address when the address begins to auto-complete. Some organisations try to limit this by disabling the auto-complete function on work emails, but that holds its own risks, where senders might mistype an email address.

For housing providers, it is worth at least considering if it is appropriate to disable the function, perhaps only for some teams, such as housing managers or allocations or rent management teams who are regularly emailing tenants or members of the public.

Email settings can also be applied to put a short delay on emails being sent, which gives the sender a window of time to realise if they have pressed send on an email to the incorrect recipient or with the wrong attachment, for example.

Employee policies on the use of email should prohibit work-related emails being sent to, or received by, an employee's personal/home email address.

This includes Board Members, who should have organisation emails, rather than using the email address from their 'day-job' or a personal email. Many housing providers, large and small, fail to set up organisation emails for Board Members, which risks sensitive emails being outside of the control of the organisation.

Clearing out both old emails and less frequently used email addresses from the autofill function should be encouraged regularly.

Where possible, sensitive information should be shared via another system, such as shared drives or encrypted email systems, rather than standard emails.

IT equipment: Laptops, etc. should be encrypted and password protected, and not left unaccompanied in public. When travelling by car laptops and other storage devices should be carried in the boot, but not left in a vehicle overnight.

Care should always be taken to make sure laptop screens can't be seen by anyone without authorisation, especially if working in public places.

Postal services: Any hard copy documents containing sensitive personal data or otherwise confidential information, for example bank details, health related information or proof of ID should be sent using recorded delivery where possible, and a 'return to sender' address should be included on the outside of the envelope.

Data breach preparation

Organisations should have a response plan that covers all data breaches and cyber incidents. This plan doesn't necessarily need to be a separate one just for personal data incidents; there's so much natural overlap between the way organisations would want to handle a loss of personal data and a loss of financial company data, for example, so it could be a plan that covers all types of important data. The data breach response plan should also be part of the overarching business continuity planning.

A data breach response plan that includes the following steps will save time and stress in the case of a data incident; Recognise, Reduce, Risk assess, Report, and Review.

To produce a robust response plan, organisations can undertake table-top exercises working through what could go wrong, and how that will impact the organisation and its customers, residents and colleagues. This type of exercise helps to highlight what sort of back-up systems might be required, and who should be on an emergency contacts list, and crisis management team.

When any breach involving personal data occurs, it should be logged and investigated, and part of the investigation and review will involve assessing whether the breach needs to be reported to the ICO; not every breach needs to be reported.

Each part of the risk framework (see chapter 9 on DPIAs) can be applied both proactively, to be prepared for data breaches and reduce their likelihood, and reactively, to be able to respond to breaches when they occur.

Proactive planning for data breaches

A proactive plan, to be prepared for data breaches and to reduce the likelihood and severity of breaches should include the five parts of this risk framework as below, to be prepared for breaches. 'Risk assessing' runs through each of the other parts of the framework, like letters through a stick of rock.

Recognise:

- Monitoring capabilities will help alert the organisation to data breaches and attacks, and to attempts too.
- An understanding of both the potential impact of types of breach – risk assessing – the organisation's risk appetite and tolerance will help determine the level of monitoring that is appropriate.

Reduce:

- Plans should include having appropriate technical and organisational controls available, that align with the potential risks and the organisation's risk tolerance levels.

Report:

- It is much easier, and less stressful, to draft at least some of the communications that will be needed in the event of a serious data breach. Even just deciding on the tone and approach, and who will be responsible for drafting and signing-off communications, can provide a good foundation when the time comes.

- Communications and reports may be required for the ICO, the Regulator of Social Housing, the public, the Board and other internal forums, customers, residents, colleagues, and stakeholders.

Review:

- The processes and controls that are designed to reduce the likelihood and severity of potential data breaches should be kept under review, so organisations need to decide how audits and reviews will be carried out, by whom, how often, and how non-compliance will be addressed.

Responding to data breaches

A response plan, to be followed in the event of a breach or incident, should also include the five parts of this risk framework as below, and it should be easily available and easy-to-follow. 'Risk assessing' runs through each of the other parts of the framework, like letters through a stick of rock.

Recognise:

- Once a breach, an attack, or an attempted attack has been identified, colleagues need to know who to contact and how to contact them, to put the response plan in motion. Contacts may include senior leaders and key colleagues, external suppliers such as IT crisis specialists (see chapter 8 on Data Processors), insurance company, the ICO, the Regulator of Social Housing.

Reduce:

- The appropriate technical and organisational measures that are available – from the proactive plans being in place – should be implemented as soon as possible in order to reduce the impact of the breach or incident. Actions can be as simple as trying to recover breached data, and may need to include continuity plans and systems, such as being able to switch to an alternative email system, telephone number, or social media accounts.

Report:

- Having already planned, and perhaps even drafted, communications and reports, having to only review and complete them allows the organisation to send them as appropriate – to the ICO, the Regulator of Social Housing, the public, the Board and other internal forums, customers, residents, colleagues, and stakeholders – more easily and quickly.

- Article 33 of the (UK)GDPR requires that every personal data breach is reported to the Information Commissioner within 72 hours of the organisation becoming aware of the breach – not the DPO or a certain individual, but the organisation in general – *"unless the personal data breach is unlikely to result in a risk to the rights and freedoms of natural persons."* (See chapter 9 on DPIAs for ways to assess the types of harms that people may suffer from incidents.)

- Data Subjects must also be informed about the data breach without undue delay *"when the personal data breach is likely to result in a high risk to the rights and freedoms of natural persons" [Art. 34 (UK)GDPR]*. However, even when the full extent of a data breach is not yet known, it can be beneficial to data subjects to inform them of a breach, sometimes even a potential breach, so that they can take preventive action and be more wary of falling victim to any scams that could arise from the breach. It can also be preferable for the organisation to be able to control the narrative to some degree and inform data subjects before they hear it from another source.

- For serious data breaches, that effect operations and customer service, the Regulator of Social Housing may need to know about the issue, as part of its regulation role.

- Even small, low-level breaches must be recorded, for trend analysis and learning, as well as accountability purposes.

Review:

- One of the most important aspects of handling a data breach, is also often missed, or not carried out as effectively as it could be; reviewing how the incident happened and how to prevent a similar recurrence. This isn't about apportioning blame, but about stopping up gaps and strengthening processes for future.

- There are a number of tools that can be used for the post-incident review, such as root and branch reviews, fishbone diagram reviews, or 'the 5 whys.'

When is a (UK)GDPR breach *not* a personal data breach?

Although the phrases "data breach" and "GDPR breach" are often used interchangeably, there is actually a difference between the two definitions.

For example, if an organisation has kept archive boxes for too long, past the point of having any justifiable reason to retain the data inside them, but the boxes and their contents have been kept safe and secure and not accessed by anyone, is this a breach?

In that situation, there's been no "data breach" as in a leak or loss of data (or of data availability), but there *has* been a breaking of the principles of the (UK)GDPR; a "GDPR breach."

It's important to differentiate between a "data breach" and a "GDPR breach" because of the confusion between the two types of breach; organisations are sometimes accused of failing to report a breach to the ICO and to the data subject in question, but only data breaches are reportable, not breaches of the GDPR principles.

It's also worth noting that, while the (UK)GDPR allows for monetary penalties to be imposed for breaching or breaking the GDPR rules and not just for security breaches, in practice the risk of being fined in the UK for anything other than a "data breach" is low. In fact, the majority of recent penalties from the ICO have not been for (UK)GDPR breaches at all, but for breaching PECR (the Privacy Electronic Communications Regulations) where companies have sent unsolicited direct marketing to individuals by electronic means, without consent.

(See chapter 14 on how the PECR rules apply to your contacts.)

Of course, this doesn't mean that a "GDPR breach" doesn't require corrective action; it's still crucial to investigate and put things right as soon as possible.

Handling complaints

Even with the best will in the world, there will inevitably be complaints from data subjects about the way their personal data is handled and processed; we will address these at the end of this section.

Other complaints, about tenancy issues or ASB (anti-social behaviour), may not seem to be a data-related complaint, but responding to it is likely to involve weighing up how much personal data can be shared lawfully.

One way to reduce the risks of divulging too much personal data, and without a lawful basis, is to 'bake-in' the rules around data sharing to all the organisation's existing complaint handling policies and procedures. This requires applying the (UK)GDPR principles and other requirements to the types of personal data that is often shared or requested when handling complaints, starting of course, with the purpose, and whether it is fair, lawful, and transparent.

One issue involved in complaints handling in social housing, that is specifically covered in the regulation is the handling of complaints received via "elected representatives". The DPA2018 Schedule 1, Part 2, paragraph 23 includes the full list of "elected representatives" that can rely on this lawful condition that comes under the sub-heading of "substantial public interest", namely *"Elected representatives responding to requests"*, but it includes members of the House of Commons, the National Assembly for Wales, the Scottish Parliament, and the Northern Ireland Assembly, as well as elected members of a county council, district council, London borough council, parish council, or community council, and more.

Personal data can be lawfully shared by an elected representative – or someone working on their behalf and with their authority – for the purposes of carrying out their functions, in response to a request by an individual to take action, such as to raise a complaint with their landlord. The landlord can lawfully share data in return, that is necessary to respond to the elected representative appropriately.

The (UK)GDPR principles also apply, of course, so any data shared must be minimal, accurate, and shared securely; this section of the law only provides the lawful basis for the sharing of necessary personal data in particular circumstances.

Sometimes, housing providers have come up against elected representatives who have asked for personal data relating to another data subject, other than the constituent they are working with. For example, they might ask what action has been taken against a neighbour of their constituent in response to an ASB complaint. In a situation like that, the necessity test is unlikely to be met.

Updating the elected representative on the progress of their constituent's complaint and similar, is more in keeping with this lawful basis.

The Housing Ombudsman published a Spotlight report on Knowledge and Information Management (KIM) in May 2023, due to a high proportion of complaints they receive being linked in some way to poor Knowledge and Information Management, or data management.

Overhauling poor knowledge and information, or data, management is far from simple, and is full of potential pitfalls, but bear in mind that many, if not all, of the strategies required to implement good data protection practices in a housing provider can also be applied to – and benefit – the management of other types of data, not just personal data.

Again, 'baking-in' the data management rules – for at least personal data handling, but it could be expanded to all data types – to the organisation's existing policies and procedures that involve the collection, use, storage, sharing, analysis, and so on, of data, is a comprehensive way to make it easier for colleagues to understand and comply with those rules.

Training sessions are of course important too – and training records can play their part in demonstrating accountability and compliance – but due to data protection law being principles based, learning what the principles say doesn't necessarily translate into improved actions.

For example, a customer service colleague could learn that the (UK)GDPR Principles require that data is only collected and used for fair, lawful and transparent purposes, but that doesn't always help during a conversation with a customer's relative. The colleague may well be left thinking "what is a fair, lawful and transparent purpose in this particular situation?"

Ideally, the organisation should translate the principles, as well as the other legal requirements, into practical terms in their policies and procedures, so that colleagues will know what data they should and shouldn't share in practice.

Complaints from individuals about data handling

Various types of complaints about data handling will likely be received by most housing providers, from those with no foundation – such as a resident complaining their data has been shared with the courts without their consent, when consent is clearly not a legal requirement in a court case – to those that are valid, when personal data has been breached or perhaps processed unlawfully.

In either case, or for anything in between, the response should be clear and concise, and written only once the relevant information has been gathered and assessed, explaining in plain-English why the processing was, or wasn't, lawful, and apologising if it was the latter.

Complaint responses must also explain to the complainant the process for escalating their complaint internally, and explain how to raise a complaint with the ICO. Some organisations are reticent about including information about the ICO complaints, but it is a legal right, and in practical terms it can help to diffuse some situations, because the organisation is being open and helpful.

Complaints from the ICO

When a complaint *does* go to the ICO, and they act on it, the organisation in question can expect an email in the first instance, from the ICO, asking for an explanation or response to the complaint. For low-level complaint, the first email will often ask that the organisation contacts the complainant directly and doesn't require a response to the ICO themselves at that stage.

Again, all responses to a complainant or the ICO should be clear and concise, although it can be more appropriate to quote article numbers to the ICO than to a data subject. It can be tempting, in responding to the ICO, to include more personal data about the complainant than is strictly necessary, which must be avoided.

CHAPTER ELEVEN

DIGITAL TRANSFORMATION IN SOCIAL HOUSING

In recent times, the term 'Digital Transformation' has become common in the social hosing sector, with the objective of improving customer experience, reducing costs, and driving sustainable growth. It's not easy, though, with so many moving parts and opportunities for things to go wrong.

In these projects, the (UK)GDPR is often seen as a potential obstacle, but with a little help, it can become the greatest asset in completing a smooth and effective digital transformation project.

Due to the pervasive misunderstanding that the key to (UK)GDPR compliance is data cyber-security – encryption, firewalls, ransomware protection, and so on – Project Managers may believe they are on top of the GDPR requirements by involving IT experts and teams in transformation projects. There may even be a worry that speaking to the data protection officer as well as the IT team will just slow down progress, because they'll just go over the same ground as the IT team.

However, because the 'protection' part of data protection is so focussed on protecting *people* from harm caused by their data being handled in a way that is unfair or unlawful, the data DPO certainly should be involved, and can be very valuable. They certainly shouldn't be going over the same ground as the IT team.

The social housing sector is of course committed to treating people fairly as part of fulfilling its social purpose, but housing providers risk failing to do this, especially when using new digital technologies or launching other projects with the potential to cause harm to individuals. And so, the DPO and the (UK)GDPR itself, can both be very valuable to digital transformation in social housing.

Any large project needs a clear purpose, otherwise there's no point in undertaking the work, and having a clear, communicated purpose help to ensure that money, time, and energy are only spent on changes that will help to fulfil a valid purpose.

The (UK)GDPR, being grounded in purpose, gives us a framework for identifying and stress-testing the purpose of a project, or any smaller part of a project.

Using two simple words – 'why?' and 'how?' – and then reviewing the answers for any potential conflict with the GDPR principles and rules, including the rights of data subjects, will highlight the validity, value, and risks, in projects.

Digital transformation projects often revolve around the introduction of new software, which is another area of risk, that the (UK)GDPR can help to control. Some vendors will recommend their software as being 'GDPR compliant', which is a misleading phrase, as there is no such thing as 'compliant software.' While there can be *features* in software that can help support compliance, no software solution can *make* data processing compliant.

The (UK)GDPR though, gives us a framework again, to ensure we avoid certain risks related to software. Security is of course crucial, but as above, it is not the only important aspect of using software.

Even if a landlord has a great relationship with a software vendor, it is placing a massive amount of trust in the vendor, by giving them the huge responsibility of storing customer or colleague personal data. Carrying out appropriate due diligence on the vendor, entering into a contract that works fairly for both parties (including controlling in which country the data can be stored), and continuing to monitor the vendor's compliance with the contract terms will reduce or control risks, and comply with the (UK)GDPR.

Digital transformation projects usually have the objective of improving the quality of the data held by the organisation, or 'cleaning' it.

'Good quality data' can be defined as data that's likely to result in benefit or success for the organisation's mission and purposes.

To achieve that success or benefit, the data held needs to be relevant, accurate, and protected (from misuse, destruction or corruption.)

Data cleansing will always involve improving the accuracy and timeliness of data, but it might not always cover ensuring the data is all relevant, so that step should not be missed out. It would be a waste of resources to spend time making sure data is accurate only to find that it's of no use to the organisation!

Of course, as we are discussing data protection here, it almost goes without saying that a valid purpose for the data should also be a fair, lawful and transparent processing purpose.

The third characteristic that makes good quality data is that it's protected.

Data is unlikely to stay good quality for long if it's too easily accessible and can be deleted or amended when it shouldn't be (either intentionally or by accident). Even worse, personal data could be misused and cause harm to the data subjects.

The principles of data protection, when applied from the very earliest stages, can provide a robust framework on which to build digital transformation projects.

CHAPTER TWELVE

CCTV AND ASB

CCTV

Many landlords use CCTV (Closed Circuit Television) to help protect property and people; customers, colleagues and members of the public. This involves collecting personal data – in the form of people's images on the CCTV footage – so the way CCTV is used must comply with the requirements of the (UK)GDPR, including upholding peoples' data protection rights. The following rules can be used to form the foundation of an organisation-specific CCTV policy, in the social housing sector.

Only use CCTV when appropriate

CCTV will not always be the most appropriate option to address an existing or possible issue and should not be the only option being relied upon. For example, security may be improved by improving fencing and lighting initially.

A Data Protection Impact Assessment (DPIA) is required to establish if CCTV is appropriate in the circumstances, and what controls are needed to reduce data-related risks. (See chapter X 9DPIAs.)

Even when it is deemed appropriate to use CCTV, its use should be kept under review, at regular intervals, or when the situation significantly changes. For example, if anti-social behaviour reduces due to a perpetrator leaving the area, it may be appropriate to remove the CCTV.

Covert CCTV

Only law enforcement agencies, including the police, have the legal powers required to use covert CCTV or other covert surveillance methods.

There may be some circumstances when the police or other law enforcement agency ask for the organisation's co-operation with a covert surveillance exercise, which should be considered on a case-by-case basis.

Selecting and siting CCTV systems

The CCTV systems used should be able to record good quality images, of the appropriate standard to be used for the purposes the CCTV is in place.

Camera positions should allow areas of interest to be filmed unobscured, but also ensure that areas that are not of interest or should not be filmed, such as private homes, are not filmed. In the rare instance that cameras can't be sited in a way that avoids filming private areas, technical solutions should be used to obscure those private areas.

The CCTV monitor positions should only allow for viewing by authorised colleagues, unless they show an area that can already be seen from where the monitor is positioned. For example, if a monitor only shows an office reception area, the monitor can be visible to anyone in that reception area.

Recorded footage should be stored securely, so it can only be accessed by authorised staff.

Use CCTV in compliance with data protection legislation

When using CCTV, the (UK)GDPR Principles must be complied with, in particular:

- Only collecting, storing and using footage with a lawful basis to do so, and telling people about how their data is being processed via the Privacy Notice and CCTV signage.

- Only collecting and using the minimum amount of footage, only using it for the specific and lawful purposes, and only keeping it for as long as is necessary.

- Keeping footage secure, in storage and when being accessed or shared.

The (UK)GDPR rights of data subjects that apply to the use of CCTV include giving people access to copies of their own data, which is – generally speaking and with exceptions – the footage that they appear in, and allowing people to ask for it to be erased. The request for erasure doesn't always need to be fulfilled though. (See chapter 6 on data subject rights.)

A third-party operating CCTV on behalf of the organisation is likely a data processor, and as controller the landlord is responsible for due diligence, processor clauses in the contract, and continuing to manage and review the contract performance. If contractors are watching the camera monitors on behalf of the landlord, the operatives must be SIA licensed.

Sharing CCTV footage

Requests for access to CCTV footage should be considered in a similar way as any other data sharing. See chapter 8 for information on data sharing.

Customer use of CCTV

Residents are increasingly using domestic CCTV, including built into doorbells, and landlords may want provide customers with guidance on the lawful use of domestic CCTV. Many adaptations policies require customers to obtain permission before mounting cameras, although this could give the impression that action will always be taken against unapproved cameras, which might not be practical. Doorbells, however, are not always covered by adaptations policies and many cameras are built into doorbells, so adaptations policies should be reviewed as appropriate for the organisation.

Advice for residents includes domestic use of CCTV is not usually subject to the data protection laws, including the (UK)GDPR. However, all users of CCTV or other recording systems should be made aware that they can make themselves subject to the law if they use the footage in any other way than for *"purely personal or household reasons." [Art. 2 (UK)GDPR.]*

The current ICO guidance recommends that members of the public should not allow their cameras to record outside of their own home's boundaries. However, based on the law itself, the way the footage is used is a clearer indicator of whether the use is for *"purely personal or household reasons"* or not. After all, an individual could film another person visiting their property, such as a courier, and be able to see their vehicle on the side of the road, but the footage could still be for their own personal or household reasons, such as being aware of visitors, and would not breach the law. Also, the use of dashcams in cars is in general lawful, as long as the footage is not misused, and clearly dashcams record outside of an individual's own home boundaries.

The law is most often breached in the use of domestic CCTV when the footage is used in a way that oversteps the boundaries of the definition of being for *"purely personal or household reasons".* Which could include publishing the footage. When this happens, the person who owns the CCTV becomes a data controller under the (UK)GDPR, with all the responsibilities that brings. A member of the public is unlikely to be able to (easily!) comply with all the legal obligations of a controller, and will therefore more than likely be automatically breaching the (UK)GDPR once they use the footage in any way that is not purely personal or household use.

Another way that domestic cameras can be problematic is when neighbours feel, and may well be, victimised and harassed by the person recording them. In an October 2021 court case, *Fairhurst V Woodard*, Mr Woodard was ordered to pay £100,000 compensation to his neighbour Dr Fairhurst after his multiple cameras and sound recording caused Dr Fairhurst to feel so uncomfortable that she ultimately left her own home. This was an extreme case, but the potential for harassment claims is real.

Receiving footage from customers

Ideally ASB policies and complaints handling policies and procedures should include information for colleagues who receive copies of domestic CCTV footage as evidence in an ASB case or a complaint. The organisation must delete copies of any footage that is not actually required as evidence.

If footage would not, or could not, be used in legal proceedings (which includes prospective legal proceedings), the data contained in the footage is subject to all the usual requirements of the (UK)GDPR, so retaining it without a lawful basis is a clear breach of the (UK)GDPR.

Once the organisation holds footage, from its own cameras or from domestic CCTV, the footage may be in scope for a Data Subject Access Request (see chapter 6 for information on DSARs.)

Anti-social Behaviour (ASB) Management

CCTV, whether managed by the landlord or a resident's or neighbour's domestic CCTV, is often used to capture evidence in ASB cases, and unfortunately it sometimes seems to incite more ASB, as neighbours have been known to 'act up' for the cameras once they know they are there.

In the main though, CCTV, as well as sound recordings, can be valuable in providing evidence to enable a landlord to take appropriate action against perpetrators.

The legal frameworks can overlap though, causing confusion. Because ASB legal cases are civil matters, the burden of proof is lower than it is in criminal cases. This gives a little more flexibility in the nature and reliability of the footage and sound recordings that can be used as evidence, in contrast to criminal cases, evidence may not be allowed if it is deemed to have been collected unlawfully.

It is vital though, for landlords, to be clear about their responsibilities as data controllers regarding CCTV footage or sound recordings. As explained above, once the landlord is in possession of the data in the format of footage or recordings, it is obliged to comply with all (UK)GDPR requirements, unless the data is being processed for the purpose of legal proceedings (which includes prospective legal proceedings).

If the data *is* being processed for legal proceedings, it is exempt from many of the standard (UK)GDPR requirements, apart from – notably – the lawfulness requirement, meaning the landlord still needs to identify a lawful basis for its processing.

CHAPTER THIRTEEN

INSIGHT AND EDI WORK

Customer Insight work

Customer insight is a key focus for many social housing providers, with the aim of better understanding their customers, to be able to better serve them.

However, there are risks if customer data is collected and analysed without regard for the (UK)GDPR. There is no such thing as 'GDPR compliant personal data' and it could be unlawful to repurpose personal, because the (UK)GDPR is purpose dependent.

Interestingly, while it's often thought that 'Data Protection' focusses on data security, in the text of the principles section of the (UK)GDPR, the word "purpose" or "purposes" is used 12 times, while the word "security" is only used once.

As an example of repurposing data for customer insight, a landlord could have customer dates of birth, collected during the application process, which *could* also be used to segment customers and indicate who might be interested in retirement living.

To repurpose the dates of birth lawfully, and safely, requires, as a start, identification of a lawful purpose for the customer segmentation from Article 6 of the (UK)GDPR.

Additionally, to comply fully with the principles, the landlord would be required to ensure it's a fair way of using the data, be transparent about it to the customers, only use the dates of birth if they are definitely accurate, set a retention timescale for the dates of birth data related to the new purpose, and, last but not least, ensure the data is kept and processed securely.

Other requirements of the (UK)GDPR in relation to this data repurposing include checking if the customer segmentation work will involve storing the date of birth data somewhere new, or in a different way, or sharing it with a new supplier, which leads to yet more questions and requirements (see chapter 8 on data processors.)

One other issue to cover off, is if the landlord wished to contact residents who it deemed might be interested in retirement living by electronic means, such as email or SMS text messages, this would only be lawful under the PECR (Privacy and Electronic Communications Regulations) if the individuals have given consent to receive such marketing messages (see chapter 14 on contacting people.)

Repurposing data has the potential to be hugely valuable, and help organisations gain insight into both customers and colleagues, but there are several steps to take in order to repurpose data lawfully, safely and with due respect for people's rights and freedoms.

Equality/Equity, Diversity & Inclusion (EDI) work

Many housing providers have EDI policies, and some organisations have produced specific menopause and/or period policies in recent times. The information that is often collected under those policies is likely to be special categories of personal data.

The implementation of a menopause or period policy might involve recording information about employees' physical or mental health, which is special categories of personal data, and therefore requires stricter controls, and the getting over of two lawful basis 'hurdles', from both Article 6 and Article 9 of the (UK)GDPR.

Most EDI policies include the recording and monitoring of certain characteristics, such as gender, age, ethnicity, religion, disability, and religion. All except gender and age are special categories of personal data under the (UK)GDPR.

A phenomenon that can be described as 'purpose paradox' can occur in the implementation of many EDI related policies. The 'purpose paradox' is when the purpose of a project or a policy, is unlikely to be achieved, because of the way it's being carried out; the 'how' doesn't align with the 'why', which results in a conflict, or a paradox.

The good news is, 'purpose paradox' can often be resolved by asking questions about the ultimate purpose, of the project or policy, and of the organisation as a whole – the 'why' – and how the implementation will work in practice – the 'how'. The how should also include some brainstorming about 'how' it might impact individuals whose data will be processed. (See chapter 9 on DPIAs for information on brainstorming the impacts of processing on individuals.)

The answers to the questions might highlight a conflict between the desired (positive) outcome and the potential (negative) impact; a purpose paradox.

Or the answers might highlight a conflict between the likelihood of the (positive) purpose being achieved, and the potential or actual costs (monetary cots, or potential harm to individuals); a negative costs/benefit calculation.

In either of those cases, the 'how' should be reviewed, and amended.

When it comes to the collection and use of personal data, especially sensitive or special categories of personal data, there are two key ways to reduce the risks to individuals; reduce and control.

Reduce the amount of data, and/or tightly control that data.

Any data that is collected under EDI related policies must of course be controlled, which includes ensuring the data processing complies with the (UK)GDPR requirements, starting with a lawful basis for the processing.

Using menopause policies as an example, if we're going to collect and use health-related data about women in our workplace who are going through menopause, we must think about the data protection principles, the rights of the data subjects to access their data and so on, and how we move that data around, who we share it with, and where we store it.

The Data Protection Principles:

- Lawful & Fair data processing – the need to identify a lawful basis for collecting & storing data (two lawful bases are required for special categories data).
- Transparent – privacy notices and other communications about how and why the data is collected and used.
- Limited purpose
- Minimal data
- Accurate and up-to-date data
- Limited data retention
- Security
- Accountability – policies, training, etc.

It is possible to lawfully collect and store health-related data under a menopause policy, if we comply with the Principles, rights, and other obligations under the (UK)GDPR.

However, if all that is putting you off a little bit, let's think about how we can support people while *100%* respecting their privacy; there are also things we can do that *don't* involve collecting any data.

Generally encourage, and allow, things that can help with some of the debilitating symptoms of perimenopause and menopause, including mood swings, brain fog, hot flushes, insomnia, and more:

- Exercise and healthy eating – Celebrations and raising money in the workplace often involve cakes and bake sales. Consider including and encouraging healthy options too. It doesn't need to be boring. A recent event had a smoothie bar and it was absolutely fantastic. The colours and the flavours and the smells – it felt like a real treat (much more so than the dried-up pastries.)

- Comfortable clothing – allow people to be a little bit more comfortable and wear what they want to wear.

- Flexible and remote working arrangements – be more flexible about times and allow teams to work from home if possible.

- Frequent breaks

- Open communication, without the information always being recorded

- Professional help – If you have colleague assistant programmes, don't make colleagues ask how to access it; make sure that everybody knows it exists, how to access it, and that it's confidential, so that nobody's sitting there thinking "I need help, but I really don't want to ask for help."

Any menopause policy or similar should include thinking about what we can put in place *without* collecting data and then where we absolutely feel we do have to collect some data, think carefully about data protection compliance.

Make sure controls are in place in your policy, which cascade down to your procedures and actions; everything that happens on the ground should be aligned to the policy and its purpose, to avoid the 'purpose paradox.'

Other EDI data collection

When considering EDI, thoughts often turn to workshops, diversity champions, EDI statistics, and so on.

There are other, quicker, actions that can support inclusion just as much, even more perhaps; considering that some of the common EDI activities can be risky and even *damaging* to inclusion.

The law does recognise the importance of processing EDI-related data though, and it is included in the list of substantial public interest lawful bases in Schedule 1, Part 1 of the DPA 2018, in two separate paragraphs:

> *"8. Equality of opportunity or treatment"* and
>
> *"9. Racial and ethnic diversity at senior levels of organisations"*

Paragraph 8 specifically allows organisations to record and monitor four characteristics – ethnicity/race, religion, health/disability, and sexual orientation – but it is lawful only if certain requirements are met; this can be achieved by following the 5 'P's:

Purpose: The purpose of the monitoring must be to maintain and/or improve equality of treatment and opportunity within the organisation, for service-users, customers, or colleagues. The purpose must not be to take action specifically regarding one or more individuals.

Policy: The organisation must have a written policy on how and why the EDI data is used.

Principles: All principles of the (UK)GDPR must be followed too, as with all data processing.

Processors: The (UK)GDPR requirements for engaging data processors, if required for the EDI data work, apply too.

Privacy enhancing: Ideally the data should be recorded anonymously, or at the very least pseudonymously, not recorded right next to the colleague's name in the HR system, or (especially not) on an uncontrolled spreadsheet. Third-party companies can be used to collect the data, and keep it anonymous from the data controller.

The first P above, purpose, means that the monitoring of EDI data should link clearly to maintaining or improving equality in the organisation. Which is easier said than done! These 4 'I's help to ensure monitoring activities are aligned with equality:

Identify the gaps/shortfall: Review the figures and compare them to national or local statistics, which may show, for example, a certain group of people are under-represented in colleagues.

Investigate why figures are showing a gap/falling short. This shouldn't be a guess or based on assumptions. For example, there may be a lack of equal opportunity or of equal treatment; people may be put off applying, or people may actually be discriminated against if they do apply for jobs.

Ideas for improvement: Specialist consultants can help with ideas for improvements; again this shouldn't be assumption-based.

Implement the agreed improvements: Not every idea will be appropriate or even possible to implement, but those that are agreed upon should be implemented and monitored.

These requirements relate specifically to the four characteristics ethnicity/race, religion, health/disability, and sexual orientation. But sex, gender reassignment, age, and marriage status are also protected characteristics under the Equality Act 2010.

While these are not "special categories" of personal data, organisations must still comply with the (UK)GDPR, which starts with having a clear purpose, and a lawful basis for the processing.

Under paragraph 9, "*Racial and ethnic diversity at senior levels of organisations*" organisations can lawfully headhunt senior leaders of specific ethnicities in order to increase diversity, but this should also be used carefully, with consideration given to all the Principles.

A few of the risks associated with some of the more commonly seen EDI activities, include:

- Colleagues asked to be diversity champions or on committees could be stressed by the extra workload on top of their day-jobs.
- Management may single out, and even put pressure on, their diverse colleagues to be the 'face' of inclusion in their workplace.
- When colleagues are asked sensitive questions, they can feel uncomfortable or even fear that they will be discriminated against.
- There's also the fact that collecting diversity data increases the security and compliance burden on the organisation.

Because collecting EDI-related data can be so complicated, and because it is by no means the only way to improve equality/equity, diversity and inclusion in practice, and possibly not even the most effective way, don't disregard the many other actions that organisations can take to increase and support EDI without risking data protection non-compliance, as they don't require the collection of any personal data at all, but still increase accessibility and inclusion.

Just a few examples include:

Using #CamelCase in hashtags to make the words clearer.

Adding 'alt. text' to images, for people using screen readers and it helps people with slow internet too, as sometimes only the alt. text will show instead of an image.

'No interruptions' rules in meetings so everyone can be heard.

Increased awareness about the risks of excluding people by using overly complicated language or making insensitive jokes.

Allowing time and places for praying, pumping breast milk, medical needs, etc. without colleagues having to ask, or being uncomfortable asking.

Reviewing job descriptions and adverts and reflecting on things such as whether applicants need to hold a driving licence or if they only need to be able to travel.

Reviewing documents and websites for clear language, easy-to-read fonts, and diverse images.

Celebrating festivals and awareness days and communicating clearly that the organisation is an ally.

All of these examples can be used alone, or alongside EDI data collection and analysis.

CHAPTER FOURTEEN

CONTACTING PEOPLE (INCLUDING PECR AND THE TSMs)

Unsolicited electronic direct marketing means any electronic communications – including email or text – sent to individuals, containing "marketing material", that they haven't specifically asked for. Anything that is not in direct response to a request for information is regarded as unsolicited and "marketing" in this context refers to more than just selling a product.

With literally thousands of customer email addresses and telephone numbers at their fingertips, it's easy for housing providers to think that a quick electronic message to everyone about their new employment support service is OK; it's not marketing because it's a free service, right?

Not necessarily and getting it wrong could be costly.

Housing associations collect a huge amount of email addresses and phone numbers from customers and potential customers over time and this data is often collected in lots of different ways and at different stages of the relationship. It's likely the organisation will then want to use these contact details to communicate quickly and at a low-cost about services such as money management, reminders of rent holidays, or about the newest shared ownership scheme.

But in brief, a landlord can't simply put all of these activities into one pot. It doesn't mean, though, that housing providers can *never* email or text their customers with news and updates.

The starting point is to assess both the purpose and content of the email. This will indicate whether it's a 'service email' and regulated by the (UK)GDPR alone, or a 'marketing email' which is regulated by both the (UK)GDPR *and* the direct marketing emails legislation PECR (the Privacy and Electronic Communications Regulations).

This informs whether that email can be sent without consent.

The difficulty that many values-led organisations, including social housing providers, have is that whilst a lot of their messages don't *feel* like marketing, as the messages aren't selling anything, they may in fact be categorised as marketing emails in the eyes of the law.

Service electronic messages

A message that is directly related to the tenancy agreement it is more likely to be a service email and not classed as "marketing".

Examples include messages about the offices being closed, an upcoming rent holiday, messages about a legally required gas check, or a change to the business structure, such as a merger with another organisation.

Feedback or market research emails are not marketing emails either, as long as they are purely for feedback and research purposes.

This type of email is regulated by the (UK)GDPR, so all the legal requirements apply, including identifying its purpose, and the lawful basis for doing it, which is likely to be that it's necessary for contract (the tenancy agreement), or in the case of feedback or research, legitimate interests. Relying on legitimate interests requires a documented legitimate interests assessment and a way for recipients to object to receiving service information via email if there is another way to receive it.

Transparency, security and – if using a processor – appropriate due diligence and processing clauses are all vital too.

"Marketing" electronic messages

If a message doesn't relate directly to the tenancy agreement and the related obligations and rights under the agreement, there's a good chance that it would be classed as marketing for the purposes of PECR enforcement.

Examples include advertising of shared ownership homes to rental customers, but also things like telling customers en masse about a money advice service, a general health and wellbeing campaign, or a fundraising campaign.

This type of electronic message is regulated by both the (UK)GDPR and PECR, so in addition to the usual (UK)GDPR requirements, PECR must be considered, and it must be considered in the first instance, because under the PECR the only applicable lawful basis is consent.

The standard of consent is as laid down in the (UK)GDPR and all emails or texts must include an option to opt out. Most bulk email services will include an 'unsubscribe' button on every email, but it can be as simple as recipients emailing back with an indication that they wish to unsubscribe (although hopefully, politely!)

There are two instances where consent is not required before sending "marketing" electronic messages.

The first is when what is known as the 'soft opt-in' applies. This applies only when an individual has bought something from the organisation or entered into negotiations to buy something from them.

For housing associations this will predominantly relate to shared ownership sales, where it would be lawful to send shared-owners marketing messages, for example about staircasing up or other properties. To be lawful though, there must be a function to allow opt-out from these types of messages, both at the point of collecting their contact details and on every subsequent email or text.

The second exception is when sending electronic marketing messages to a business, including if the contact is along the lines of 'firstname.surname@company.com'.

The PECR regulations do not require consent before sending 'business to business' (B2B) emails, whether they are for the purposes of marketing or stakeholder and partnership working. For "marketing" messages though, the organisation's identity must be apparent from the message, and there must be a clear opt-out facility.

Non-marketing messages to businesses will likely rely on the lawful basis of legitimate interests – with a documented legitimate interests assessment – which does mean recipients have the right to object to the processing, but if it's not marketing, and the messages were valid work-based messages, it is unlikely an objection request would stand.

Managing consent

It's easy to say 'manage consent' but hard to do, especially as it's not lawful to email or text people to request permission to email or text them with "marketing" messages!

Obtaining consent will quite possibly require a concerted effort, using awareness campaigns and existing customer touch-points, and collecting fresh consent from new customers too, but it is worth it, as the penalties for breaching the PECR are currently up to £500,000 monetary penalties. In the last couple of years the vast majority of monetary penalties imposed by the ICO have been for breaches of the PECR rather than the (UK)GDPR.

It's worth noting that when outsourcing the sending marketing messages, if the emails or texts are sent without valid consent, and are in breach of the PECR, the controller is still likely to be held responsible by the ICO, as the instigator of the messages. Buying in email lists is also fraught with problems as consents cannot be verified.

Oh, and putting 'this is a service message' at the top of a marketing email isn't going to make that true! Even one 'drop' of marketing in a message can turn that message into a marketing message for the purposes of the PECR.

Marketing that does not come under the PECR, such as sending out hard copy letters, will usually meet the "legitimate interests" lawful basis, but if anyone objects to receiving marketing, even hard copies, the processing of their data for sending that marketing must be stopped immediately.

Regulator of Social Housing Tenant Satisfaction Measures:

The Regulator of Social Housing (RSH)'s new Tenant Satisfaction Measures (TSM) were published in 2022 and the data collection started in April 2023 in social housing providers across the country.

While it's good to see in the RSH guidance a warning against publishing TSM results that might identify individuals, for reasons of confidentiality, this is only a part of data protection.

Registered Providers collecting data for the TSM should consider controls for before, during, and after the data collection.

Failing to cover off these points risk non-compliance with the (UK)GDPR, including from the risks of transferring data to a country or company without adequate safeguards in place, complaints about actual or perceived misuse of data, and having excess data released if/when a data breach happens, as examples.

Guidelines for landlords collecting data for the TSM include: ensuring customers understand why and how TSM data will be used, and including TSM in the Records of Processing; building processes to ensure all the data collected for the TSM is relevant, accurate, only used for the TSM, and not kept for too long; and that it is kept in a secure manner and published in a way that preserves individuals' confidentiality.

CHAPTER FIFTEEN

WHAT NEXT?

There are a lot of aspects to data protection compliance in social housing, enough to fill several books over, but the first step to robust data protection is to stay calm (easier said than done!)

The second step is to never lose sight of the fact that data protection is about purpose, not just security.

It is not always recognised that data protection actually relates to at least 90+ percent of what goes on in the social housing sector.

There are opportunities to demonstrate how wide-reaching and ever-present the use of personal data is in social housing, though, and there are opportunities to demonstrate that good data protection practises can be an asset, not an obstacle.

Even tricky issues in housing that aren't as closely linked to personal data, such as the golden thread requirements of the Building Safety Act can benefit from applying the data protection principles as a framework and starting point for robust data management, or as the Housing Ombudsman called it knowledge and information management.

This is the process I follow myself when faced with a data protection query:

1. Ask "why?" (sometimes several times over!) to understand the desired outcome of the processing.

2. Ask "how?" to understand if the plan will likely achieve the desired outcome, or if there any immediate risks or high costs, even before considering the principles and lawful bases. The answers to these

two questions sometimes result in a different plan, and the processing won't go ahead.

3. Only when it is clear the processing is going ahead, I consider the lawful basis, then the risks as they relate to other principles, data subject's rights, and the GDPR rules around transferring data, to work out what controls or actions I'm going to recommend.

4. And often, to help get my thoughts in order, I speak with trusted colleagues in the wonderful data protection community!

MORE BOOKS BY LAW BRIEF PUBLISHING

A selection of our other titles available now:-

'A Practical Guide to Estate Administration and Crypto Assets' by Richard Marshall
'A Practical Guide to Managing GDPR Data Subject Access Requests – Second Edition' by Patrick O'Kane
'A Practical Guide to Parental Alienation in Private and Public Law Children Cases' by Sam King QC & Frankie Shama
'Contested Heritage – Removing Art from Land and Historic Buildings' by Richard Harwood QC, Catherine Dobson, David Sawtell
'The Limits of Separate Legal Personality: When Those Running a Company Can Be Held Personally Liable for Losses Caused to Third Parties Outside of the Company' by Dr Mike Wilkinson
'A Practical Guide to Transgender Law' by Robin Moira White & Nicola Newbegin
'A Practical Guide to 'Stranded Spouses' in Family Law' by Mani Singh Basi
'A Practical Guide to Residential Freehold Conveyancing' by Lorraine Richardson
'A Practical Guide to Pensions on Divorce for Lawyers' by Bryan Scant
'A Practical Guide to Challenging Sham Marriage Allegations in Immigration Law' by Priya Solanki
'A Practical Guide to Legal Rights in Scotland' by Sarah-Jane Macdonald
'A Practical Guide to New Build Conveyancing' by Paul Sams & Rebecca East
'A Practical Guide to Defending Barristers in Disciplinary Cases' by Marc Beaumont
'A Practical Guide to Inherited Wealth on Divorce' by Hayley Trim
'A Practical Guide to Practice Direction 12J and Domestic Abuse in Private Law Children Proceedings' by Rebecca Cross & Malvika Jaganmohan
'A Practical Guide to Confiscation and Restraint' by Narita Bahra QC, John Carl Townsend, David Winch
'A Practical Guide to the Law of Forests in Scotland' by Philip Buchan
'A Practical Guide to Health and Medical Cases in Immigration Law' by Rebecca Chapman & Miranda Butler

‘A Practical Guide to Bad Character Evidence for Criminal Practitioners by Aparna Rao
‘A Practical Guide to Extradition Law post-Brexit’ by Myles Grandison et al
‘A Practical Guide to Hoarding and Mental Health for Housing Lawyers’ by Rachel Coyle
‘A Practical Guide to Psychiatric Claims in Personal Injury – 2nd Edition’ by Liam Ryan
‘Stephens on Contractual Indemnities’ by Richard Stephens
‘A Practical Guide to the EU Succession Regulation’ by Richard Frimston
‘A Practical Guide to Solicitor and Client Costs – 2nd Edition’ by Robin Dunne
‘Constructive Dismissal – Practice Pointers and Principles’ by Benjimin Burgher
‘A Practical Guide to Religion and Belief Discrimination Claims in the Workplace’ by Kashif Ali
‘A Practical Guide to the Law of Medical Treatment Decisions’ by Ben Troke
‘Fundamental Dishonesty and QOCS in Personal Injury Proceedings: Law and Practice’ by Jake Rowley
‘A Practical Guide to the Law in Relation to School Exclusions’ by Charlotte Hadfield & Alice de Coverley
‘A Practical Guide to Divorce for the Silver Separators’ by Karin Walker
‘The Right to be Forgotten – The Law and Practical Issues’ by Melissa Stock
‘A Practical Guide to Planning Law and Rights of Way in National Parks, the Broads and AONBs’ by James Maurici QC, James Neill et al
‘A Practical Guide to Election Law’ by Tom Tabori
‘A Practical Guide to the Law in Relation to Surrogacy’ by Andrew Powell
‘A Practical Guide to Claims Arising from Fatal Accidents – 2nd Edition’ by James Patience
‘A Practical Guide to the Ownership of Employee Inventions – From Entitlement to Compensation’ by James Tumbridge & Ashley Roughton
‘A Practical Guide to Asbestos Claims’ by Jonathan Owen & Gareth McAloon
‘A Practical Guide to Stamp Duty Land Tax in England and Northern Ireland’ by Suzanne O’Hara
‘A Practical Guide to the Law of Farming Partnerships’ by Philip Whitcomb
‘Covid-19, Homeworking and the Law – The Essential Guide to Employment and GDPR Issues’ by Forbes Solicitors
‘Covid-19 and Criminal Law – The Essential Guide’ by Ramya Nagesh

'Covid-19 and Family Law in England and Wales – The Essential Guide' by Safda Mahmood
'A Practical Guide to the Law of Unlawful Eviction and Harassment – 2nd Edition' by Stephanie Lovegrove
'Covid-19, Brexit and the Law of Commercial Leases – The Essential Guide' by Mark Shelton
'A Practical Guide to Costs in Personal Injury Claims – 2nd Edition' by Matthew Hoe
'A Practical Guide to the General Data Protection Regulation (GDPR) – 2nd Edition' by Keith Markham
'Ellis on Credit Hire – Sixth Edition' by Aidan Ellis & Tim Kevan
'A Practical Guide to Working with Litigants in Person and McKenzie Friends in Family Cases' by Stuart Barlow
'Protecting Unregistered Brands: A Practical Guide to the Law of Passing Off' by Lorna Brazell
'A Practical Guide to Secondary Liability and Joint Enterprise Post-Jogee' by Joanne Cecil & James Mehigan
'A Practical Guide to the Pre-Action RTA Claims Protocol for Personal Injury Lawyers' by Antonia Ford
'A Practical Guide to Neighbour Disputes and the Law' by Alexander Walsh
'A Practical Guide to Forfeiture of Leases' by Mark Shelton
'A Practical Guide to Coercive Control for Legal Practitioners and Victims' by Rachel Horman
'A Practical Guide to Rights Over Airspace and Subsoil' by Daniel Gatty
'Tackling Disclosure in the Criminal Courts – A Practitioner's Guide' by Narita Bahra QC & Don Ramble
'A Practical Guide to the Law of Driverless Cars – Second Edition' by Alex Glassbrook, Emma Northey & Scarlett Milligan
'A Practical Guide to TOLATA Claims' by Greg Williams
'A Practical Guide to Elderly Law – 2nd Edition' by Justin Patten
'A Practical Guide to Responding to Housing Disrepair and Unfitness Claims' by Iain Wightwick
'A Practical Guide to the Construction and Rectification of Wills and Trust Instruments' by Edward Hewitt
'A Practical Guide to the Law of Bullying and Harassment in the Workplace' by Philip Hyland

'How to Be a Freelance Solicitor: A Practical Guide to the SRA-Regulated Freelance Solicitor Model' by Paul Bennett

'A Practical Guide to Prison Injury Claims' by Malcolm Johnson

'A Practical Guide to the Small Claims Track – 2nd Edition' by Dominic Bright

'A Practical Guide to Advising Clients at the Police Station' by Colin Stephen McKeown-Beaumont

'A Practical Guide to Antisocial Behaviour Injunctions' by Iain Wightwick

'Practical Mediation: A Guide for Mediators, Advocates, Advisers, Lawyers, and Students in Civil, Commercial, Business, Property, Workplace, and Employment Cases' by Jonathan Dingle with John Sephton

'The Mini-Pupillage Workbook' by David Boyle

'A Practical Guide to Crofting Law' by Brian Inkster

'A Practical Guide to the Law of Domain Names and Cybersquatting' by Andrew Clemson

'A Practical Guide to the Law of Gender Pay Gap Reporting' by Harini Iyengar

'NHS Whistleblowing and the Law' by Joseph England

'Employment Law and the Gig Economy' by Nigel Mackay & Annie Powell

'A Practical Guide to Noise Induced Hearing Loss (NIHL) Claims' by Andrew Mckie, Ian Skeate, Gareth McAloon

'An Introduction to Beauty Negligence Claims – A Practical Guide for the Personal Injury Practitioner' by Greg Almond

'Intercompany Agreements for Transfer Pricing Compliance' by Paul Sutton

'Zen and the Art of Mediation' by Martin Plowman

'A Practical Guide to the SRA Principles, Individual and Law Firm Codes of Conduct 2019 – What Every Law Firm Needs to Know' by Paul Bennett

'A Practical Guide to Adoption for Family Lawyers' by Graham Pegg

'A Practical Guide to Industrial Disease Claims' by Andrew Mckie & Ian Skeate

'A Practical Guide to Redundancy' by Philip Hyland

'A Practical Guide to Vicarious Liability' by Mariel Irvine

'A Practical Guide to Applications for Landlord's Consent and Variation of Leases' by Mark Shelton

'A Practical Guide to Relief from Sanctions Post-Mitchell and Denton' by Peter Causton

'A Practical Guide to Equity Release for Advisors' by Paul Sams

'A Practical Guide to Financial Services Claims' by Chris Hegarty
'The Law of Houses in Multiple Occupation: A Practical Guide to HMO Proceedings' by Julian Hunt
'Occupiers, Highways and Defective Premises Claims: A Practical Guide Post-Jackson – 2nd Edition' by Andrew Mckie
'A Practical Guide to Financial Ombudsman Service Claims' by Adam Temple & Robert Scrivenor
'A Practical Guide to Running Housing Disrepair and Cavity Wall Claims: 2nd Edition' by Andrew Mckie & Ian Skeate
'A Practical Guide to Holiday Sickness Claims – 2nd Edition' by Andrew Mckie & Ian Skeate
'Arguments and Tactics for Personal Injury and Clinical Negligence Claims' by Dorian Williams
'A Practical Guide to Drone Law' by Rufus Ballaster, Andrew Firman, Eleanor Clot
'A Practical Guide to Compliance for Personal Injury Firms Working With Claims Management Companies' by Paul Bennett
'RTA Allegations of Fraud in a Post-Jackson Era: The Handbook – 2nd Edition' by Andrew Mckie
'RTA Personal Injury Claims: A Practical Guide Post-Jackson' by Andrew Mckie
'On Experts: CPR35 for Lawyers and Experts' by David Boyle
'An Introduction to Personal Injury Law' by David Boyle

These books and more are available to order online direct from the publisher at www.lawbriefpublishing.com, where you can also read free sample chapters. For any queries, contact us on 0844 587 2383 or mail@lawbriefpublishing.com.

Our books are also usually in stock at www.amazon.co.uk with free next day delivery for Prime members, and at good legal bookshops such as Wildy & Sons.

We are regularly launching new books in our series of practical day-to-day practitioners' guides. Visit our website and join our free newsletter to be kept informed and to receive special offers, free chapters, etc.

You can also follow us on Twitter at www.twitter.com/lawbriefpub.

www.ingramcontent.com/pod-product-compliance
Lightning Source LLC
LaVergne TN
LVHW022050200926
848481LV00003B/850
9781916698215